Cornell Studies in Industrial and Labor Relations
Number 21

The Miners' Fight for Democracy

Arnold Miller and the Reform of the United Mine Workers

by Paul F. Clark

New York State School of Industrial and Labor Relations
Cornell University

Cover design by Michael Rider
Cover photo by Earl Dotter/American Labor

Library of Congress number: 81-2011
ISBN: 0-87546-086-0 (cloth)
ISBN: 0-87546-087-9 (paper)

Library of Congress Cataloging in Publication Data

Clark, Paul F., 1954–
  The miners' fight for democracy.

  (Cornell studies in industrial and labor relations;
no. 21)
  Includes index.
  1. United Mine Workers of America—History.
2. Miller, Arnold, 1923–   . I. Title. II. Series.
HD6515.M615C5   331.88′122′0924 [B]   81-2011
ISBN 0-87546-086-0   AACR2
ISBN 0-87546-087-9 (pbk.)

Copies may be ordered from

New York State School of
Industrial and Labor Relations
Cornell University
Box 1000
Ithaca, New York 14853

To my parents and my wife

Contents

Acknowledgments

This work is the result of an intense interest in the United Mine Workers and the reform movement of the Miners for Democracy that developed from the opportunity I had to work in the research department of the UMW in 1975. The intensity, sense of purpose, and dedication of the miners and staffers who joined the effort to reform and revitalize the coal miners' union, and whom I had the privilege to meet and work with, have provided the incentive necessary to carry this project to completion.

My initial interest in labor history and union administration, as well as my early efforts on this topic, were stimulated and encouraged by Professor Maurice F. Neufeld of the New York State School of Industrial and Labor Relations, Cornell University. Thomas Kochan of the Massachusetts Institute of Technology and Andrew W. J. Thomson of the University of Glasgow, Scotland, read parts of this manuscript; and Thomas C. Woodruff, formerly UMW research director and executive director of the President's Commission on Pension Policy, and Lois Gray, associate dean of the School of Industrial and Labor Relations, Cornell University, read the entire manuscript. I am grateful for their suggestions and assistance.

My primary debt is to Professor Roger Keeran of the School of Industrial and Labor Relations, Cornell University. His inexhaustible patience in reading numerous drafts of this work and his insightful criticism and advice have shaped and improved the final product immeasurably. Throughout the process, he has remained a friend.

Financial assistance and time to complete the project were provided by the School of Industrial and Labor Relations, Cornell University, and by the Department of Labor Studies at Penn State University. Without their help this work would not have been possible.

The libraries at Cornell, the University of Pittsburgh, and

West Virginia University were valuable resources in the writing of this manuscript. The staffs at these libraries were most helpful.

The final draft was typed by Debi King and Lois Nowicki, who transformed the rough drafts into a finished product while retaining their good humor. Holly Bailey and Frances Benson of the Publications Division of the School of Industrial and Labor Relations guided the manuscript through the editing and production processes with a cheerful enthusiasm that made the experience a pleasure.

Lastly, thanks are due to the person whose contribution to this effort was undoubtedly the greatest, my wife Darlene. She stoically endured the typing and retyping of rough drafts, the late nights, and the misspent weekends. It is her shoulder I have leaned on the hardest.

While I acknowledge the contributions that many people have made to this work, I alone bear responsibility for any errors or shortcomings.

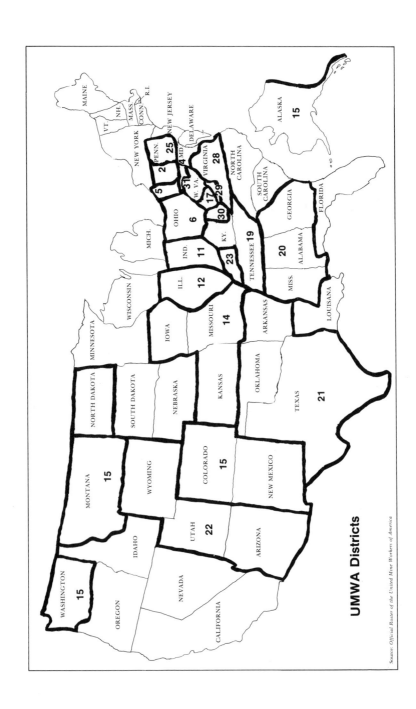

UMWA Districts

Source: *Official Roster of the United Mine Workers of America*

Introduction

O_N December 31, 1969, gunmen hired by United Mine Workers (UMW) president Tony Boyle shot and killed Jock Yablonski, a reform candidate for UMW president in the 1969 election, his wife, and daughter as they lay in their beds. Twenty-nine months later, on May 27, 1972, nearly five hundred rank-and-file coal miners gathered at a convention in Wheeling, West Virginia, to carry on the struggle Yablonski had begun. Banded together in an organization called Miners for Democracy (MFD), the group succeeded in unseating the incumbent Boyle in the government-monitored election of 1972. Much has been written about the Yablonski tragedy and the MFD movement; however, the insurgency itself would have been just a curious phenomenon if its goals and aspirations were not pursued and achieved. The purpose of this work is to document the progress, achievements, problems, and dynamics of the MFD-inspired Miller administrations that governed the UMW from 1972 to 1979.

The fate of the democratic reform movement in the mine workers' union is worthy of examination because of its potentially far-reaching influence. Labor organizations are above all "instruments of interest representation."[1] If a union is to be responsive to the interests of its membership, then that membership must have, without endangering the vital functions of the union, maximum access to and involvement in the decision-making process of that organization. Democracy is the most effective means of guaranteeing that an organization will accurately and consistently represent the interests of the collective

1

membership, something the UMW leadership had failed to do. For this reason democracy became the mechanism through which dissenting miners hoped to remake their union.

Without question, the reform efforts of Arnold Miller had great effect on the structure and function of the UMW as an organization. This influence, and the changes the new leadership made in wages, benefits, and working conditions in the coal industry, affected every one of the nearly two hundred thousand coal miners in the union. The reform experience of the UMW, an organization that had always been considered in the vanguard of organized labor, was watched very closely by the rest of the American labor movement. The successful election bid of the reform group within the miners' union led many to hope, and many to fear, that MFD was only the beginning of a larger movement within American labor, a movement in which the rank and file in other unions would band together to challenge the established leadership. The influence of the Miller reform administration went even beyond the bounds of organized labor. The American energy industry generally, and specifically the coal industry, were not unaffected by the dramatic changes taking place within the UMW. The effects the union's new leadership would have on labor stability, costs, and productivity would greatly influence coal's role in America's critical energy picture. This examination of the UMW's experience during the Miller years is intended to shed light on what was, as well as what could have been.

The conditions that spurred Jock Yablonski, and subsequently the MFD, to challenge the regime of Tony Boyle, have their roots in the history of the UMW; Chapter 1 is an historical introduction to the underlying dynamics of the movement for a more democratic UMW. Chapter 2 looks at the Miller administration's initial efforts at reform during its early days in office and at the 1973 UMW convention. The union's completely redesigned collective bargaining process and the first contract negotiated by the reform administration are examined in Chapter 3. The transition from corrupt kingdom to a rank-and-file democracy was a torturous process, and the difficulties and problems encountered by the reform program are the focus of Chapter 4. Chapter 5 examines the process and progress of the important

1976 UMW convention. The last months of the Miller adminis-tration and the 1977 international elections are examined in Chapter 6. Chapter 7 discusses the early years of Miller's second administration, including the 1977–78 contract talks. Chapter 8 reports on the 1979 convention, and Chapter 9 reviews, in light of the aspirations of the reform movements, the accomplish-ments and failures of the Miller years.

1 Prelude to Reform: The Union before Miller

J OCK Yablonski's election challenge and murder and the Miners for Democracy (MFD) convention in Wheeling were the seeds of what would prove to be a successful revolution in the United Mine Workers (UMW). This revolution was spurred by the policies and practices of the Lewis and Boyle regimes. The savage response that Yablonski drew and that MFD escaped because of court supervision of their election bid merely reflected the values, customs, and accepted mores that guided the organization under the leadership of John L. Lewis and Tony Boyle. It would be impossible to understand the turbulent years of change and reform without first understanding something about the circumstances that preceded, and in essence were responsible for, the reform movements of 1969 and 1972.

The United Mine Workers of America originated in 1890 when the National Progressive Union of Miners and Mine Laborers, formerly the National Federation of Miners, and the miners' group within the Knights of Labor merged at a founding convention held in Columbus, Ohio. During its first thirty years, the union was racked by inconsistent leadership as eight different men held the office of UMW president. Except for the period from 1898 to 1907, when John Mitchell's leadership brought some stability to the organization, the UMW struggled to survive and mature in the midst of the hard-fought organizing wars of the late nineteenth and early twentieth centuries.[1]

In 1919, John Llewellyn Lewis, then the appointed vice president of the union, assumed the presidency of the UMW when President Frank Hayes resigned because of poor health. Elected in his own right by a narrow margin in January 1921, Lewis would not relinquish the reins of power for more than forty years. During these years, Lewis systematically transformed the UMW into a labor autocracy with himself at the head.[2]

The union that John L. Lewis inherited in 1919 was a largely decentralized confederation in which actual power and authority resided more at the district level than at international headquarters. It was inevitable, therefore, that Lewis's efforts over the years to centralize the union would meet with resistance from the powerful district leaders who jealously guarded their authority and, in many cases, had expansionary ambitions of their own. The challenges Lewis faced during his early years in office were led by three individuals: Alex Howat of District 14 (Kansas), Frank Farrington of District 12 (Illinois), and John Brophy of District 2 (Pennsylvania). During this turbulent period, Lewis used a vast array of tactics and strategies, sometimes of dubious morality and legality, to respond to these men and the opposition groups they led.[3]

Lewis's initial challenge came at the UMW convention of 1921. This was his first opportunity to contest his opponents' authority, and it came at a time when Lewis's hold over the presidency was still very tenuous and his struggle for mastery of the union had just begun. Lewis chose this occasion to confront Howat, a militant district leader who ran his district independent of the policies and directives of the international. Earlier in the year, Howat had sanctioned a strike over a grievance in his home district without first exhausting the avenue of union-management consultation. This was violation of the UMW's contract with the district operators. On these grounds, Lewis called for Howat's suspension from union office, a recommendation endorsed by a roll call vote of the convention. This was Lewis's first major triumph at a union convention.

After the suspension of Howat, Lewis sent in one of his own lieutenants to administer the district. The defeat of Howat's appeal at the 1922 convention amplified Lewis's initial victory.[4]

In 1923, opposition to Lewis emerged when left-wing rank-and-filers met in Pittsburgh to form the Progressive Miners International Committee (PMIC). Although affiliated with the American Communist Party's labor arm, the Trade Union Educational League (TUEL), PMIC members also retained their membership in the UMW. The PMIC drew up a socialist-inspired platform, and in 1924 supported a candidate against Lewis in the international elections. The candidate, George Voyzey, a Communist miner from Illinois, lost badly to Lewis who used red-baiting tactics and dual-unionist charges to discredit the dissident candidate and his organization.[5]

In the mid-twenties only one district president, Frank Farrington of District 12 (Illinois), showed any semblance of independence from Lewis. Undoubtedly, Lewis viewed Farrington's autonomy as a roadblock to his consolidation ambition. Farrington, a man not unlike Lewis in his approach to union leadership and politics, however, seemed secure in his job and beyond Lewis's reach. Nonetheless, in August 1926, Lewis forced Farrington's resignation from office and permanent ouster from the union under circumstances which, even today, remain somewhat mysterious. Lewis accomplished this coup by exposing a secret pact Farrington had signed with Peabody Coal Company in July 1926. The pact made the Illinois district leader a "labor advisor" to the company for the considerable fee of $25,000 a year. By making public this clandestine agreement, Lewis effectively and permanently destroyed Farrington's reputation among miners everywhere. The manner by which the UMW president became aware of this contract and obtained a copy of it, when the original was locked in the company's Chicago vault, has never been fully explained.[6]

Although Lewis consistently beat back challenges to his administration and destroyed those who resisted his authority, opposition continued to arise in the mid-twenties as the UMW suffered contract defeats and membership losses from employer offensives. In late 1926, John Brophy, a former District 2 president and longtime dissident, entered the race for UMW president in opposition to Lewis. Running on a Save the Union theme, Brophy's platform included nationalization of the mines, aggressive organizing, and the creation of a labor party.[7] Because of his progressive platform and tacit alliance with the trade union Communists, Brophy was an obvious target for Lewis's red-baiting strategy. With this antired, antiradical message being spread across the coalfields by the UMW president's many patronage appointees, Brophy faced long odds in his bid to unseat Lewis.[8]

When the tellers reported the election results in December 1926, Lewis had won with 170,000 votes to Brophy's 60,000, a high margin of victory even for a well-entrenched incumbent like Lewis. Brophy was suspicious of the results and charged Lewis with widespread election fraud and vote stealing. Brophy secured affidavits documenting that the official returns for several locals in District 2 differed substantially from the actual local returns reported to the union's tellers. He also charged that the reported returns of District 20 (eastern Kentucky), 2,686.5 votes for Lewis out of a potential 2,686.5, were incredible and highly unlikely. Brophy believed these instances were only the tip of the iceberg. Despite his documented allegations, the International Executive Board (IEB) rubber-stamped the election report of Lewis's tellers.[9] Thirty-eight years later, Brophy wrote in his autobiography, *A Miner's Life,*

> Nobody can ever prove who won the election of 1926, because the evidence can never be secured. Those reports that were not falsified in the locals were taken care of by agents of the international office. But the vote-stealing is so obvious and flagrant in the official report itself that the inference that Lewis would not have won without stealing votes is a defensible one.[10]

This accusation, and all the circumstances surrounding the Brophy election challenge, show the lack of restraint in Lewis's efforts to retain and consolidate his power as head of the UMW. Vote stealing, red-baiting, and political blackmail all played integral parts in Lewis's empire-building approach to leadership.

By 1927, John L. Lewis had succeeded in destroying or neutralizing most of his serious rivals in the union, including Alex Howat, Frank Farrington, and many of those associated with

7

the PMIC. He had smashed Brophy's election challenge and within a year stripped him of his UMW membership on grounds of dual unionism, a charge Lewis used to destroy the Save the Union opposition movement that remained in 1928.[11] At this point, relatively secure in his power and position, Lewis moved to consolidate his kingdom. To this end, he employed the convention mechanism to institutionalize his authority and legitimize his one-man rule through the trappings of quasi-constitutional due process.

Constitutionally, the UMW convention was designed as a check and balance on the power of the administration.[12] Vested with supreme authority by the constitution, the union convention served as the arena in which the leadership must account to the membership. Lewis, however, never recognized this function of the convention; he treated it simply as a power struggle to be won or lost. UMW historian McAlister Coleman's description of a typical early Lewis convention, before all significant opposition had been interred, illustrates well Lewis's approach and the chaos that accompanied it:

> Following the opening prayer and address of welcome by the mayor the first order of business was to have the Chairman instruct the sergeant at arms to eject Powers Hapgood and other insurgents from the hall. Then amid boos and derisive whoops from the opposition, Lewis would read his report for the year.... With every sign of perturbation William Green ... would read his treasurer's report skipping hurriedly over the miscellaneous section.... The chair would then refuse official recognition of Alex Howat, who would come charging down the middle aisle to scramble over the press table onto the platform. Whence he would be hurled back by administration supporters.... Lewis would boom his defiance of the opposition.
>
> "May the chair state," he thundered at the Indianapolis convention of 1924, "that you may shout until you meet each other in hell and he will not change his ruling?"
>
> "For what purpose does the delegate arise?" Lewis would ask an objector.
>
> "I want to go on record ..."
>
> "If you want to go on record, write it on a slip of paper and hand it to the secretary. Next business."[13]

Once he had largely subdued his opponents, however, Lewis was able to transform the convention into a travesty of personal testimonials, backslapping, and rubber-stamping that served only to solidify the president's control. Thus, beginning in 1927, Lewis conventions became much more sedate but even more farcical in terms of democratic process than the convention described by Coleman. It was in these conventions that Lewis institutionalized his abuse of power.

Facing a largely loyal delegation at the 1927 convention, Lewis routed what little opposition remained. Taking on his outnumbered progressive rivals in votes on several issues, the UMW president won a 50 percent salary increase for himself and a free hand to levy assessments on the membership to furnish funds for his IEB. Lewis also won a crucial weapon when, at his behest, the convention voted to bar Communists from membership in the UMW. Lewis's mastery of the 1927 convention was so complete that in the course of the meeting not a single section of any report failed to pass.[14]

Lewis took the opportunity his dominance of the convention presented to warn publicly that the union's leadership would not tolerate dissent and opposition. Focusing on John Brophy's recent election challenge, and particularly on Brophy's public statements that under Lewis's leadership the UMW had become weak and vulnerable, the eloquent Lewis castigated the dissident with his finest rhetoric:

> In the days when people were besieged in a walled city and a soldier got upon the top of the wall and called to the enemy that the people were weak, they merely took his life and threw him off the wall to the dogs below. Here in these modern times we tolerate the lamentations of the timid and we even tolerate at times the words of a traitor ... (however) I say ... that the man who stands upon this platform and mouths mutterings of consolation to the enemies of this Union is nothing more nor less than a traitor.[15]

With this statement on February 2, 1927, Lewis made it clear that, in the future, even more than in the past, opposition to his leadership would equal treason. The message was clear and

9

effective. John L. Lewis would never again face a serious challenge in a UMW election.

After the 1927 convention and the death of the Save the Union movement in 1928, Lewis, having driven out or expelled all his rivals, faced no threat within the miners' union. Although men like Howat, Farrington, and Brophy continued to oppose him, this opposition necessarily emanated from outside the UMW. This rivalry proved an irritant to Lewis, but had little effect as he opportunely seized the threat of outside enemies to further solidify and expand his powers. This was the case in 1930, when many of Lewis's old antagonists allied to form a new miners' union, the Reorganized United Mine Workers (RUMW).[16]

Led by Howat, and supported initially by Brophy, the RUMW dissidents asserted that the present UMW leadership had allowed the union to formally dissolve by failing to hold the scheduled convention of 1929. In order to reconstitute the union, the RUMW held a convention in Springfield, Illinois, in March 1930. From the start, disunity and discord plagued the meeting. Early in the proceedings, John Brophy withdrew his support of the movement when the convention voted to give delegate credentials to the dishonored Frank Farrington. The RUMW was not a national insurgent movement. From its inception it had been dominated by and composed largely of Illinois (District 12) miners, despite Howat's leadership position in Kansas and Brophy's in Pennsylvania. Of the 467 delegates in Springfield, 325 (70 percent) were Illinoisans.[17] A group with such a narrow base could hardly expect to gain legitimacy and acceptance on a national scale. The RUMW, rocked by dissension and limited in its appeal, never achieved its lofty aspiration of displacing John L. Lewis.

To counter the RUMW rump convention, Lewis convened the 1930 UMW convention in Indianapolis on the very day, March 10, that the dissident meeting began. With the ousted dissident leaders and a large proportion of the rank and file hostile to Lewis assembled in Springfield, Lewis faced an almost totally loyal delegation at his convention. Taking advantage of this, he won even broader powers and control over the union than he had enjoyed in the past. Once again every committee report and resolution passed without exception. Specifically, the convention authorized Lewis to "interpret the meaning of the International Constitution and to exercise unrestrained executive power between meetings of his IEB."[18] In addition, the delegates broadened the president's power to expel members for fomenting dissent and dual unionism. Most significantly, however, Lewis gained the power to revoke the charters of districts, subdistricts, and locals and to create provisional governments to administer their affairs.[19] Although Lewis had employed trusteeship to a limited extent in his political wars of the twenties, he had been forced to use this drastic measure sparingly and with restraint as it lacked constitutional legitimacy.[20] With the passage of a constitutional amendment granting him this power, Lewis received the weapon with which he would deliver the deathblow to democracy in the UMW.

Lewis emerged from the 1930 RUMW skirmish more firmly in command and control of the miners' union than ever before. As in 1927, Lewis had profited immensely from the convention, demonstrating once again the importance of the union convention in the building of Lewis's labor autocracy. Throughout this period Lewis used the convention to defeat and destroy his enemies, to expand his power and authority, and to shroud his actions in constitutional legitimacy. Some of Lewis's victories, as those over Farrington and Brophy, occurred as a result of Lewis's skills in politics and power outside of the convention. In most cases, however, Lewis institutionalized the power he gained and the methods he used—trusteeships, election review, expulsion of members—through the convention.

From the mid-1930s on, Lewis conventions were orchestrations lacking any authenticity as democratic assemblies. One of the keys to Lewis's dominance of this crucial democratic process lay in his control over the convention's committees. Committee appointments were political boodle that Lewis handed out with great skill. Since convention committees played such a key role in the convention proceedings, Lewis's political loyalists inevitably manned the committees. His men on the rules committees placed in Lewis's hands as much control over the proceedings as possible. His appointees on the credentials com-

11

mittee, the three international auditors who had run on the Lewis ticket, controlled the composition of the delegation and could rule invalid the credentials of any dissident and seat large numbers of staff people and delegates from ineligible but loyal locals. The appointments he would make to the important committees on scale (wages and bargaining), constitution, and resolutions usually assured Lewis control over the nature and quantity of substantive issues that would be raised in the course of a given convention. In the twelve conventions chaired by Lewis after 1936 not a single roll call vote occurred. This symbolized the inertia and paralysis of the convention mechanism in the coal miners' union.[21]

After the convention of 1930, the RUMW survived for a few years, and a handful of other dual miners' unions arose to oppose the UMW establishment. But Lewis's power and resources, the onslaught of the Great Depression, and the active and ruthless opposition of employers to any union, particularly one more militant than Lewis's, combined to destroy or render insignificant all alternatives to the UMW. The weak and fractious RUMW fell apart and was succeeded in Illinois by the Progressive Mine Workers of America, a dual union of small membership and little significance.[22] At the same time a number of Socialist and Communist veterans of the Save the Union movement made renewed efforts to form alternative miners' unions.

Frank C. Keeney organized the West Virginia Mine Workers Union in 1931 and almost immediately led a strike of that state's twenty thousand miners. The realities of life in West Virginia in the thirties—powerful coal operators, company towns, and a captive state government—crushed the strike and the new union. Communist trade unionists across the coalfields abandoned all hope of "boring from within" and formed a separate National Miners Union (NMU) in 1931. Centered in western Pennsylvania, eastern Kentucky, and Ohio, the NMU quickly gained more members in those regions than the UMW. As with Keeney's union, however, its policy of action and militancy and the power of the operators and government led to its destruction. By 1933, these attempts to challenge Lewis's autocracy from outside had failed.[23]

The years from 1920 to 1933 were years of trauma and decline for the United Mine Workers, as they were for the entire American labor movement. Much as a nation's leader is granted increased authority and power in time of emergency, Lewis opportunistically grabbed authority and power during this time of crisis. This centralization was the root for the revolt that would eventually occur in the UMW. The election of Franklin D. Roosevelt in 1932, however, marked the nadir of the period of economic decline and the beginning of the long period of economic revitalization in American society. John L. Lewis, now firmly in command of the UMW, seized this rejuvenation to advance the cause of American coal miners through the process of collective bargaining. His success in this arena stemmed any opposition within the union for many years to come.

At the time of Lewis's death in 1969, the *New York Times* described John L. Lewis as "a pugnacious man of righteous wrath and rococo rhetoric."[24] At no time was this more true than during the contract battles of the thirties and the forties, when Lewis reached the peak of his eloquence and his arrogance. During these years Lewis did not make proposals at the bargaining table, he made demands. He did not argue or plead with the coal operators, he attacked them, scorned them, and assaulted them with his finest rhetoric—nor did he do this behind closed doors. Rather he made his case in headlines where all the world and all the miners could see it. Lewis described his efforts to the miners this way:

> I have never faltered or failed to present the case of the mine workers of this country. I have pleaded your case not in the quavering tones of a feeble mendicant asking alms, but in the thundering voice of the captain of a mighty host, demanding the rights to which free men are entitled.[25]

This was the Lewis style, at least during the years of his bargaining successes.

Lewis's headfirst approach to collective bargaining won more than headlines. On September 21, 1933, he signed the bituminous coal code provided for under the new National Industrial

Recovery Act (NIRA).[26] This code granted the UMW something it had long sought—a contract covering the major portion (70 percent) of the national bituminous coal tonnage. This national agreement was a tremendous improvement over the chaos that had previously existed under the old system of regional bargaining. The economics of the industry, thousands of small producers in a wide geographic area, necessitated the central control of policy and strategy this form of bargaining allowed. Yet the consequence of this arrangement was that control of the collective bargaining process, including the formulation of demands and the decision to strike, passed from the local to the international level. This extended the top-down decision-making process within the union to the most vital and immediate area of membership concern.[27]

For the coal industry, the thirties were a period of recovery. Despite the infirm state of the industry, Lewis extracted small but symbolically important wage increases from operators anxious to cut miners' wages. The most important concession that Lewis won during the thirties, however, was the union shop. Granted by the Appalachian Operators' Association in 1939, the union shop offered security and strength as the UMW prepared itself for the years ahead when the industry would be healthy and the deferred gains of the depression could be recaptured.[28]

World War II and the mobilization effort in the United States brought almost immediate prosperity to the American economy and to the nation's coal trade. The boom presented a new opportunity for the UMW to press its demands on a healthy industry. Despite the resistance of the operators, the condemnation of the president of the United States, and the vitriolic opposition of the public, John L. Lewis pressed his demands during the wartime period. Included among his gains were substantial wage increases, in the forms of pay hikes (16 percent in 1941) and portal-to-portal pay (payment for time enroute to the place of work within the mine), and the extension of the union shop to those few mines owned by steel companies (captive mines) and not yet covered.[29]

Lewis's finest performance as a negotiator and probably his greatest victory at the bargaining table occurred during this era with the establishment of the UMWA Welfare and Retirement Funds in 1946.[30] The Funds, financed by the payment of a royalty by the employer on each ton of coal mined, helped to fill the void in health care and social welfare that existed in the isolated and backward coalfield communities of postwar United States. The humanitarian potential for relieving suffering that the newly created medical benefits, miners' hospitals, and pensions possessed was great. The decline in coal production during the fifties and the accompanying decline in income for the Funds, poor management, and a wavering commitment of the UMW to its brainchild caused the Funds to operate with only varying degrees of efficiency during their thirty-year history.[31]

Lewis and the miners fought hard for these gains; the price was high, both in wages and in public sympathy lost. Between 1934 and 1952 there were thirty-four major work stoppages in the coalfields, including eleven industrywide strikes.[32] These strikes led the government to seize the mines on five occasions.[33] UMW members, however, sacrificed more than lost wages and the public's goodwill to win these great victories. They also relinquished any control they still possessed over their union and its officers. Throughout this period, with the centralization of bargaining authority in the office of the president, Lewis directed policy, strategy, and mobilization like a field marshall directing his troops. The effects of this one-man control and the blind obedience that permitted it, while initially positive, would be devastating to hundreds of thousands of coal miners and to the entire region of Appalachia in the years to come.

During this period, the UMW did have a bargaining structure that dated back to at least 1932.[34] The structure was quasi-formal, since it had no constitutional basis or authority; it was a customary procedure legitimized by its acceptance and continued observance. At each convention the president appointed a national wage scale committee to handle resolutions dealing with collective bargaining matters. As explained to the 1938 UMW convention by Vice President Thomas Kennedy, it was "the duty of the National Wage Scale Committee to use these resolutions as a basis for the proper determination of (the union's) demands. . . ." in negotiations with the coal operators.[35] In all

15

probability, the wage scale committee only reviewed any contract resolutions submitted and made recommendations on potential contract demands to Lewis.

In addition to the convention's National Wage Scale Committee there was the standing National Wage Policy Committee, composed of international officers and district representatives and "clothed with authority to deal with all matters in the making of . . . basic wage Agreement(s)."[36] In theory, this committee was to oversee the negotiation of all contracts and also had the responsibility of approving these agreements. One of Lewis's biographers, Saul Alinsky, however, was probably close to the truth when he wrote in 1949 that the "union policy committee is a mere rubber stamp as is everyone else in the union."[37]

The UMW's internal processes for contract negotiations during the thirties and forties were simple. When an agreement was due to be renegotiated or when John L. Lewis felt an agreement should be renegotiated, he would assess the situation and formulate contract demands. Lewis would then present his demands to the coal operators in his finest bellicose style. Next, he would proceed to bargain with them, casting Shakespearean jibes at appropriate moments. When impasse was reached, Lewis would command his troops to lay down their tools and man the picket line, which they did without question. When Lewis was satisfied with the terms he would accept the operators' offer and present it to the men who had to live with it.

This description is not far from the reality of Lewis's day. Though the bargaining process involved other individuals in supporting roles, one man made the decisions. Lewis justified his omnipotent role in bargaining to Saul Alinsky: "I work harder than anyone else in this union, and I know more about the problems of the miners than anyone else. Therefore, I should think that my decisions would mean more than those of anyone else."[38] Without question, they did.

The signing of the National Bituminous Wage Agreement in March 1950 signaled the beginning of a new era for the UMW. This shift was marked by a sudden reversal in Lewis's relationship with the coal operators he had tormented for so long.

Symbolic of this shift was Lewis's cooperation with the operators on the issue of mechanization in the industry. In retrospect, it appears highly questionable that his shift in approach
was in the best interests of the union's membership.

Without a doubt, the coal industry of the fifties was in
trouble. The American fuel market had shifted during the
postwar period. Oil and gas had begun to heat homes and
diesel fuel to power locomotives. From 1940 to 1964, coal's
share of the industrial energy market in the United States fell
from 30.3 percent to 23.1 percent, and its share of the retail
energy market dropped from 19.6 to 4.6 percent.[39] To improve the industry's competitive position the coal operators
looked to increased productivity. Mechanization, and the reduced labor costs that would accompany such a process, was
one obvious answer to the productivity problem. Although the
economic benefits of mechanization were potentially great, so
was the human cost of jobs lost as men were replaced by
machines.

When Lewis began his period of collaboration in 1950,
416,000 men worked as coal miners. By 1959, his last year in
office, only 180,000 men remained at work in the coalfields,
the drop largely a result of the free hand to mechanize the
mines Lewis granted the operators throughout the fifties.[40]
When asked, shortly before his retirement in 1959, about the
trend toward mechanization, Lewis proudly declared,

> The United Mine Workers not only cooperated with the
> operators on that—we invented the policy. We've encour-
> aged the leading companies in the industry to resort to
> modernization in order to increase the living standards of
> the miner and improve his working conditions.[41]

Lewis justified this action on the grounds that

> it is better to have half a million men working in the
> industry at good wages and high standards of living than
> it is to have a million working in the industry in poverty
> and degradation.[42]

While it can be argued that Lewis had a practical responsibility
to the welfare of the industry that employed his members, it

17

was the welfare of his members in the industry and not the industry itself that was his first responsibility. His actions had a dramatic effect on UMW coal miners across the country.

By 1964, close to three hundred thousand miners had lost their livelihood, at least partly as a result of Lewis's acquiescence. Although mechanization may have been necessary and inevitable, as Lewis argued, the UMW president did little to ease the adverse effects of this process on his membership. The coal companies introduced machinery rapidly and with little regard for the men the machines displaced. Lewis did nothing to prevent this and, even worse, nothing to cushion the blow these former union brothers received. No retraining programs or rehabilitation programs were established for those thrown out of work. In many cases the union cut benefits from the Welfare and Retirement Funds that the unemployed or prematurely retired miners needed desperately. Also during this period, the union first decided to shut down, then to sell, the medical facilities it had built and supported throughout the coalfields.[43] The industry discarded thousands of union miners, and the UMW looked the other way.

The UMW leadership compounded the trauma of the fifties by engaging in numerous questionable financial transactions. These transactions included large investments in coal companies and utilities that, in some cases, resulted in the loss of millions of dollars of mine workers' dues and Funds money.[44] At the same time, the union's leadership cooperated in sweetheart deals with the large coal operators aimed at driving the smaller coal operators, who were less able to pay union wages and benefits, out of business.[45] The courts of the sixties and seventies found both of these practices to be unlawful; the bad investments constituted a "breach of trust" on the part of those responsible for the Funds' money, and the sweetheart cooperation violated the federal antitrust statutes.[46] The centralized decision-making process within the UMW, conceived and developed by Lewis, contributed greatly to the conditions that permitted such malfeasance to go unchecked.

The new approach to collective bargaining that Lewis unveiled in 1950 carried over the concentrated responsibility for negotiations that he had previously enjoyed but went a step further in removing the rank and file from the negotiations process of their contract. Previously, Lewis carried out negotiations with much fanfare and publicity, enabling the membership to have at least a limited awareness of what was occurring. The method of bargaining that arose in 1950 came to be known as "mystery bargaining," after the clandestine manner in which Lewis reached agreements.[47] The talks consisted of two-man sessions, Lewis and an operators' representative, conducted in strict privacy. Since agreements reached after 1950 were open-ended, having no expiration date, and since the parties allowed no publicity when contract talks began, no one except the men negotiating knew when a new contract was being formulated. When Lewis and the operators' representative reached a new agreement, the wage policy committee quietly assembled to give it their seal of approval. Not until the pact was final and binding did Lewis inform the membership of its provisions.[48]

Great tyrants, jealous of their power, often surround themselves with men much less capable than themselves, men who are not a threat to their kingdom. The result is often disastrous. When John L. Lewis stepped aside in 1960 at the age of eighty, Thomas Kennedy, the elderly UMW vice president, succeeded him. The new vice president and heir apparent was W. A. ("Tony") Boyle, a top aide to Lewis since 1947. When Kennedy died in early 1963, Boyle, at the age of fifty-eight, became the eleventh president of the union. One-time president of the Montana coal miners, Boyle had held the job of assistant to the UMW president for twelve years. In that capacity, he "executed a host of ill-defined and covert duties," all of which taught him the Lewis approach to union administration.[49] Once in power, Boyle coveted the same authority and control for his administration that he had seen Lewis wield during his later years in office. Since the mechanisms of power had been so thoroughly institutionalized by Lewis, it was simple for Boyle to assume the same authority.

Under Tony Boyle, the neglect and unresponsiveness of the UMW leadership continued as corruption spread throughout the organization. Open discontent over wage agreements negotiated by Boyle emerged as miners slipped behind their coun-

19

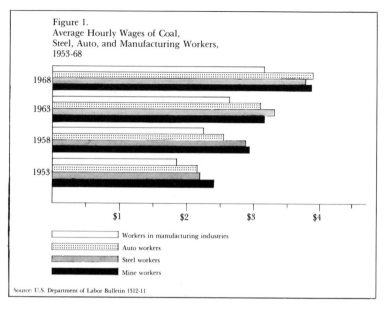

Figure 1.
Average Hourly Wages of Coal,
Steel, Auto, and Manufacturing Workers,
1953-68

Workers in manufacturing industries
Auto workers
Steel workers
Mine workers

Source: U.S. Department of Labor Bulletin 1312-11

terparts in the steel and auto industries (see figure 1).[50] Coal operators, sensing a weak and pliable union leadership, took advantage of the situation to stagnate safety and health reforms, violate contract provisions, and ignore grievance procedures. With unemployment high and job security low, non-union operators successfully fought the weak organizing efforts of the union and, in some instances, launched successful union-busting drives.[51]

Boyle continued and, in many instances, exacerbated the abuse of power within the union that had begun under Lewis. Nepotism, for instance, riddled union hiring practices. Boyle appointed his daughter, Antoinette, to a $40,000-a-year job as UMW attorney in Montana; the job was sufficiently undemanding that she was able to maintain her private practice as well. Boyle's brother Dick, joined the payroll for $25,000 a year as the appointed president of District 27 in the western states. International Secretary-Treasurer John Owens's family also profited from union jobs as two sons took home $40,000 and $25,000 a year in staff salaries.[52]

Taking care of relatives did not cause the union officers to neglect their own comfort. During nine years in office, the Boyle administration spent considerable sums of miners' dues money on indulgences and luxuries. The leadership maintained a fleet of three Cadillac limousines for its transportation and, in John Owens's case, a suite at Washington's Sheraton-Carlton Hotel as a residence. Owens's suite alone cost the UMW membership $70,000 over a six-year period.[53]

The most blatant financial impropriety committed by Boyle during his years in office involved a special pension fund he set up for "resident International officers." Boyle and Secretary-Treasurer Owens transferred $650,000 from the union's treasury to a special account to guarantee pensions at full pay for life. Without the consent or even the knowledge of the UMW's executive board, Boyle and Owens planned and implemented this elite arrangement, for which only they and John L. Lewis qualified.[54]

Boyle discovered in his early days in office that while it might be possible to exercise the authority and control institutionalized by Lewis, he could never assume the almost superhuman proportions that Lewis had assumed in miners' eyes. Whereas Lewis's demigod image allowed him in his later years to escape dissent and criticism, Boyle faced opposition from the start. Under Lewis, opposition had come to equal treason, and Boyle had learned to deal with it as such. The new leadership's repression tactics first emerged openly at the 1964 UMW convention.

At great expense to the union, Tony Boyle chose to hold his first convention in Bal Harbour, Florida, thus breaking a long UMW precedent of holding conventions in cities located in or convenient to the major coalfields (Columbus, Ohio; Pittsburgh, Pennsylvania; Washington, D.C.).[55] During his twelve years as Lewis's aide, Boyle witnessed convention after convention where the delegation showered the president with adulation and rubber-stamped administration proposals like clockwork. In order to assure that this occurred at his convention, Boyle, with an eye on his upcoming election later in the year, orchestrated a costly show of support, complete with bands playing songs of praise and gifts for all delegates stamped with Boyle's name and likeness. The price of such a display was high; the bill for bands alone exceeded $390,000. Patronage constituted an important part of the proceedings. Boyle appointed fifty-two men to an appeals and grievance committee at a salary of $1,457 each, though the convention did not consider a single appeal or grievance—nor did the 1964 convention confront any significant issues. From the start, dissenters who criticized Boyle met with physical intimidation and, in more than one case, Boyle strong arms used force to silence opposition.[56] For Boyle, the convention was not the supreme decision-making body of the union but rather an opportunity to buy support with a sunny and exotic clime, trinkets, political appointments, and hard cash.

The 1968 convention repeated the performance of 1964. Instead of going south, Boyle flew virtually the entire delegation from the Appalachian, central, and southern coalfields to Colorado. Instead of functioning as a constitutional device to review and check the power of the leadership, the convention at Denver again witnessed blatant violations of the UMW constitution by its president. Delegates were paid inflated amounts to cover their expenses without furnishing receipts as constitutionally required. Bogus locals, without a shred of legitimacy or even an effort to cover their illegality emerged.[57] Whereas Lewis had manipulated the convention to make constitutional provisions for his excessive power and had cloaked his abuses behind rigged convention approval, Boyle assumed the excesses without any concern for even conjured legitimacy.

In the area of collective bargaining it was business as usual. The UMW signed four contracts during Boyle's nine years in office. In each case—1964, 1966, 1968, and 1971—Boyle negotiated in the style developed by Lewis during the fifties. Talks took place between Boyle and an operators' representative behind closed doors. The same rituals of internal process were observed, allowing for the same amount of rank-and-file involvement—virtually none.[58]

In the early sixties, however, events signaled a changing attitude of miners toward their union and particularly toward the all-important bargaining process. Massive walkouts, occurring after the signing of an agreement, not during its negotiation, were aimed in protest at the union leadership, as well as the employer, and symbolized this change. The first significant incident of this type occurred after the contract settlement of

March 1964 when eighteen thousand miners struck for eighteen days to protest the agreement Tony Boyle had signed with the operators. This demonstration took place not in protest of the basic wage increase of two dollars a day negotiated by the UMW leadership, but rather in opposition to the lack of fringe benefits, pension increases, and improvement in health and safety provisions in the final settlement. Again in April 1966, miners across the country refused to return to work for seventeen days due to their dissatisfaction with the Boyle-negotiated agreement. As in 1964, the strikers, this time forty thousand of them, anticipating healthy gains in all areas of the contract as the industry recovered from the slump of the fifties, were disappointed with Boyle's settlement. This trend continued in 1971 when rank-and-file miners called a short protest strike after the signing of that year's contract. As in previous years, a lack of improvement in fringe benefits and safety spurred the walkout.[59]

The new outlook of at least some of the UMW's rank and file, as revealed by these demonstrations, had its roots in the traumatic events of the fifties. Changing conditions, however, helped to guide membership dissatisfaction into rank-and-file action. The passage of the Labor-Management Reporting and Disclosure Act (Landrum-Griffin Act) of 1959 and the highly publicized hearings leading up to its passage, undoubtedly affected the way members viewed their union leadership. The idea that labor unions had a legal obligation to guarantee certain inalienable rights to their members within the organization, including the rights of dissent and free speech, was new to the members of John L. Lewis's union. In addition, the passing of the reins of power from a demigod to a man of less stature certainly made an impression on miners resigned to following the great Lewis.

The opposition that arose eventually took the form of a democratic reform movement. Although scattered rank-and-file activism arose in the form of protest strikes during the early and middle sixties, the beginnings of the democratic reform movement can be traced to two separate events, the Farmington mine disaster of 1968 and the black lung strike of 1969. In November 1968, Consolidation Coal Company's Number 9 mine in Farmington, West Virginia, exploded, killing seventy-eight miners. Boyle arrived at the scene and in an interview before the television cameras said, "As long as we mine coal, there is always this inherent danger." He added that Consolidation Coal was "one of the best companies to work with as far as cooperation and safety are concerned."[60] The spectacle of the union president defending the safety practices of a coal company while seventy-eight miners lay buried in the mine below probably convinced many UMW members that the interests of the miners had been forgotten by the leadership.

The Farmington disaster and the Federal Coal Mine Health and Safety Act pending in Congress brought national attention to the issue of the health and safety of coal miners in late 1968 and early 1969. At about the same time, a group of coalfield doctors, I. E. Buff, Donald Rasmussen, and Sonny Wells, along with rank-and-file organizations like the Black Lung Association, a West Virginia–based group, began to agitate for black lung legislation to compensate the victims of pneumoconiosis, or black lung, a disabling occupational disease common in coal miners and linked to the inhalation of fine coal dust. These groups criticized the UMW for its lax attitude toward such legislation. When the issue went before the West Virginia State Legislature in 1969 in the form of a union-supported bill, the black lung groups opposed it and lobbied for a stronger measure that made it easier for victims to obtain benefits. When the legislature balked at passing the stronger measure, a spontaneous wildcat strike, opposed by the union but involving 95 percent of the state's miners, swept West Virginia. The strike lasted twenty-three days and ended only after the legislature acceded to the miners' demands and enacted one of the most enlightened worker's compensation laws in the country.[61]

The black lung victory of 1969 had a profound effect on many coal miners discontent with their union. The smoldering resentment born in the fifties broke into open anger over the Farmington explosion and the union leadership's reaction to it. The black lung movement convinced many that their anger could be channeled into effective action. Their victory demonstrated that the rank and file could challenge and defeat the union leadership. These factors—combined with the improving employment conditions that ended the layoffs in the industry and brought an influx of young, militant individuals into the mines, a result of the coal companies' need to hire more workers to keep their mines in compliance with the new federal health and safety act—provided hope for reform. In the wake of this optimism, Jock Yablonski made the decision to launch his challenge to the Boyle regime. The encouragement of friends and family and the influence of social activist Ralph Nader, who had taken a strong interest in the corruption of the Boyle administration and in the issue of health and safety in the coal industry, were crucial factors in Yablonski's decision to run for the UMW presidency.[62]

Yablonski announced his candidacy for the presidency of the mine workers' union on May 29, 1969, in Washington, D.C., at the Mayflower Hotel. Yablonski said at that time, "I do so out of a deep awareness of the insufferable gap between the union leadership and the working miners that has bred neglect of miners' needs and aspirations and generated a climate of fear and inhibition."[63] Yablonski himself had been a part of that leadership for years, serving as IEB member from District 5 in western Pennsylvania since 1942 and as district president for eight years. He explained his defection from the union bureaucracy:

> They've sat on their backsides so long they've let the fat come up between their ears and they don't know what the coal miner's problems are anymore.[64]

He also stated that

> when I see my union moving in a direction of unconcern for men who have to engage in the dangerous conditions of coal mining, then it's time that somebody speaks up . . . regardless of what the sacrifice may be![65]

Yablonski was not a rank-and-file miner. When he announced his election challenge he had been out of the mines for more than twenty-five years. But many miners involved in the burgeoning rank-and-file movement felt that with a man of Yablonski's stature on their side they had a much better chance of unseating Boyle. Thus the rank-and-file reform activists gave Yablonski their full support. When stacked up against the massive strength of the union's administration, his grass roots campaign faced tremendous odds. In counteracting this disadvantage, one of his greatest strengths was the platform on which he would run. Yablonski pledged a return of democracy to the UMW and promised to restore autonomy to all of the union's districts. In addition, pledges to end the corruption and nepotism and to make health and safety reforms a high priority brought him much support among working miners.[66]

Throughout the campaign of 1969 Yablonski's attorney, Joe Rauh, citing numerous illegalities on Boyle's part, including "threats to Yablonski's supporters, improper use of the *UMW Journal* for campaign purposes, and irregularities in local union nominating meetings," requested Department of Labor intervention in the election.[67] The department refused all Rauh's requests, and on December 9, 1969, the reform movement suffered its first setback when Tony Boyle defeated Jock Yablonski by a vote of 80,751 to 45,736.[68] Twenty-two days after the election, on December 31, 1969, Boyle's hired gunmen entered the Yablonski home in Clarksville, Pennsylvania, and murdered Jock Yablonski, his wife, and daughter in their beds. On January 8, 1970, the government officials who had spurned Yablonski's calls for help until then, belatedly ordered a full investigation of the election. On May 1, 1972, the Department of Labor overturned the 1969 election, citing massive irregularities, and ordered a new election with full government supervision.[69] The former union president would soon be convicted of murder and sentenced to three consecutive life terms in prison.[70]

At Jock Yablonski's funeral, miners who had worked with Yablonski during the election challenge decided to form a new organization, Miners for Democracy (MFD), to carry on the struggle in which Yablonski had fallen. The movement, initially led by rank-and-file miner Mike Trbovich, gained strength as other rank-and-file organizations, such as the Black Lung Association and the Disabled Miners and Widows of Southern West Virginia, both active in the 1969 black lung strike, threw their support behind Miners for Democracy. A cadre of lawyers who had been actively involved in the Yablonski campaign played an important role fighting MFD's battles in the courts. The group included Yablonski's sons, Chip and Ken, and Joe Rauh, and they eventually succeeded in winning a rerun of the 1969 election as well as other legal victories against the Boyle forces. These legal victories, combined with the hopes of reform activists, kept the rank-and-file movement alive through 1970 and 1971.[71]

After the federal courts overturned the 1969 election, MFD began laying plans for the new election. On May 27, 1972, MFD held its nominating convention at Wheeling, West Virginia. Opened to all UMW rank-and-file coal miners, and attended by close to five hundred, the meeting named a slate of candidates to oppose Boyle in the December elections. The MFD slate included presidential candidate Arnold Miller, forty-nine years old; vice presidential candidate Mike Trbovich, fifty-one years old; and secretary-treasurer candidate Harry Patrick, forty-one years old.[72]

MFD's selection of Arnold Miller to head the reform group's challenge to Tony Boyle surprised many people. As the *New York Times* reported, "Running for the union's presidency seems a role for which Mr. Miller, a soft-spoken, curly-haired, lantern-jawed descendent of Anglo-Saxon migrants to the Appalachians, is not naturally endowed."[73] Miller, the son of a union coal miner, was born near Cabin Creek, West Virginia, on April 25, 1922. Having finished the ninth grade, he entered the mines at age sixteen. After serving in the Army and being severely wounded at Normandy in World War II, Miller returned to the mines in 1951 as a repairman and electrician. Suffering from arthritis and black lung, Miller was forced into a disability retirement in 1970.[74]

Arnold Miller had served one year as a UMW local president and, at the time of his nomination, was president of the Black Lung Association. Unlike his predecessor Jock Yablonski, however, Miller did not have significant experience in union administration or politics when he began his run for the UMW's top post. But he quickly demonstrated his aptitude for union politics by putting enough votes together at the nominating convention to upset the preconvention favorite, Mick Trbovich.[75] He accomplished this by using his Black Lung Association involvement as a political base and by gaining exposure in the months before the convention by working actively on behalf of the MFD cause. Another factor favoring his nomination is suggested by rumors that some MFD leaders were concerned about the viability of a candidate with an eastern European name. If true, this could have given Miller an edge over Trbovich.[76]

Trbovich gracefully accepted the number-two spot on the reform group's ticket. A working miner from Clarksville, Pennsylvania, the MFD candidate for vice president had close ties to the Yablonski candidacy, having served as Jock Yablonski's campaign manager. This, and Trbovich's twenty years of experience as a local union officer, undoubtedly made him a valuable asset to MFD's slate. The MFD candidate for secretary-treasurer was Harry Patrick, a mine mechanic from Barrackville, West Virginia. Like Miller, he had little experience as a union leader. At age forty-one, Patrick was the youngest member of the reform team.[77]

In addition to nominating its slate of candidates, the MFD convention passed a reform platform that demanded the restoration of district autonomy, including the right to elect district officers and representatives; the overhaul of the union's administration, including the cutting of salaries and officers' pensions and the practice of nepotism; the establishment of a bill of rights for members; and a greater emphasis on such basic membership priorities as safety, health, and organizing.[78]

The MFD campaign of 1972 had three advantages that Yablonski did not have in 1969. First, the entire campaign and election were conducted and supervised according to strict regulations laid down by a federal judge and enforced by the Department of Labor. Voting occurred over an eight-day period from December 1 to December 8, allowing labor department observers to supervise voting in every local union.[79] In addition, the court order opened the *UMW Journal* to opposition candidates, authorized slate balloting, and required candidates to file financial reports. Second, MFD benefited from the large influx of young miners who entered the mines between 1969 and 1972 as prosperity returned to the industry. In his dissertation, Paul Nyden has estimated that there were 37,214 more young miners in union mines in 1972 than when Yablonski ran in 1969. Accepting his assumption that most young miners supported MFD and given the relatively small margin of MFD's victory, it is very possible that young miners had a decisive influence in the 1972 election.[80]

A third contributory factor was the litigation the Boyle administration had experienced since the last election. Along with legal proceedings that eventually overturned the 1969 election, a group of miners and miners' widows sued Boyle and the UMW in 1969 for improprieties in the administration of the Welfare and Retirement Funds. A United States district court decided this case in April 1971, finding the Funds, including the UMW and Boyle, guilty and disqualifying Boyle as a fund trustee.[81] The courts handed down their most damaging verdict in March 1972, when Boyle was found guilty on thirteen counts in connection with illegal campaign contributions made with union funds.[82] Although this decision was appealed, Arnold Miller faced a convicted felon in the 1972 runoff for UMW president. This, combined with other suits and indictments, gave Miller an advantage that Yablonski never had.[83]

By December 17, the early tabulations showed Miller with a decisive lead over the incumbent. A few days later the official count revealed that Arnold Miller had defeated the incumbent Tony Boyle by a margin of just over fourteen thousand votes, Miller receiving 70,373 to Boyle's 56,334. Returns also showed that Mike Trbovich, Harry Patrick, and six other candidates running for positions as international teller and auditor on the reform ticket had won.[84]

MFD campaign staffer Tom Bethell described the reform slate's inauguration as UMW international officers after the election victory:

> The Labor Department certified Miller's election December 20; two days later the president-elect sat in a Washington courtroom and listened as Judge Bryant made the election official. It had been nearly 3 years to the day since the first moves had been made to void Boyle's 1969 election; now there was triumph.
>
> A few minutes later Miller walked across the grass of McPherson Square, headed through the open doors of the Mine Worker's Building, across the lobby—past a

Table 1   Results of the 1972 UMW Presidential Election

District	Miller	Boyle
2 Central Pennsylvania	5465	5396
3 Western Pennsylvania	217	522
4 Western Pennsylvania	2967	2184
5 Western Pennsylvania	5567	3315
6 Ohio	6384	2112
10 Washington	84	152
11 Indiana	1089	2157
12 Illinois	6830	3860
14 Iowa, Missouri, Kansas	410	514
15 Colorado, New Mexico	935	912
17 Southern West Virginia	7583	4853
19 Central Kentucky, Tennessee	594	2454
20 Alabama	1144	4170
21 Arkansas, Oklahoma, Texas	135	574
22 Utah, Arizona, Wyoming	909	1251
23 Western Kentucky	2204	3376
25 Eastern Pennsylvania	9170	1845
27 Montana	123	273
28 Virginia	4127	2913
29 Southern West Virginia	6544	6566
30 Eastern Kentucky	2144	3374
31 Northern West Virginia	5681	3343
Totals	70,373	56,334

Source: *UMW Journal*, December, 1972, p. 3.

small Christmas tree and a large glowering bust of John L.—and down a flight of steps to the large basement room where the inauguration was to take place. Suddenly there was pandemonium as hundreds of miners, already jammed into the room, jumped to their feet, cheering, singing, yelling, crying. Miller, who is normally the most composed of men ("colorless", *Life* magazine called him, misunderstanding him) found himself moist-eyed and turned away, embarrassed. But there was nothing to be embarrassed about, and in the swearing-in ceremonies that followed, Harry Patrick gave way to tears and laughter all at the same time. He wasn't the only one.[85]

The MFD victory marked the first successful, rank-and-file challenge to the UMW hierarchy in the union's history. The *New York Times* went as far as saying that "nothing like it had ever happened in the labor movement before."[86] In a sense it was true. A movement of idealistic but inexperienced, little-educated, rank-and-file coal miners had taken over the leadership of one of America's most powerful and important labor organizations. But as soon as the movement had won its election victory the question of whether this same group of rank-and-file miners could transform the UMW into a democratic organization by implementing the platform it had passed at its 1971 Wheeling convention, let alone administer a complex, widespread labor union and bargain successfully with a multi-million-dollar industry, became paramount.

2 Early Days of the Administration: The 1973 Convention

THE officer's report to the 1973 UMWA convention describing the progress, programs, and activities of the reform administration's first year in office was appropriately titled *The Year of the Rank and File, 1973*. Fresh from its election victory in 1972, the new administration led by Arnold Miller pushed ahead enthusiastically with efforts to reform the union as it had promised. But, as the reformers soon learned, they could not accomplish change overnight. The first year of the reform administration was almost entirely consumed in cleaning house and laying the foundation upon which a democratic United Mine Workers could be built.

At the time of Miller's election in December 1972, twenty of the twenty-four district representatives to the International Executive Board were Boyle appointees; only four districts retained the right to elect their representatives. Three hours after taking office on December 22, 1972, Miller removed all twenty of the Boyle-appointed IEB members. He then appointed interim board members in thirteen of the districts until district elections for the positions could be held. The adminis-

tration left six IEB positions vacant, also pending district elections. A court-ordered election held at the same time as the
Miller-Boyle election filled the remaining IEB slot left vacant
by a Boyle appointee.[1]

The new administration took advantage of the period preceding IEB elections to initiate its program of reform. The
dominance of Miller appointees, combined with the momen-
tum of the successful reform movement and election, created a
cooperative atmosphere between the president and the IEB
that, although short-lived, was very productive. This unanimity
of purpose allowed Miller to progress rapidly with his house-
cleaning of Boyle abuses, policies, and staff.

One of the first important measures was the removal of
Boyle loyalists from union staff positions. In the weeks immediately following his installation as UMW president, Miller fired
Edward Carey, UMW general counsel under Boyle; Suzanne
Richards, assistant to Boyle; Antoinette Boyle, a union attorney; and numerous minor staffers in the safety, education,
and organizing departments and in various district offices. To
fill many of the major staff vacancies, Miller appointed a number of nonminer activists who had assisted him in the 1972
campaign. Included among these initial appointees were Chip
Yablonski as UMW general counsel; Rick Bank as executive
assistant to the president; Don Stillman as director of publications; Ed James as executive assistant to the president; and
Meyer Bernstein as director of public and international affairs.
In filling numerous other positions, Miller named rank-and-file
miners active in the Miners for Democracy movement.[2]

In its first month in office, the reform administration also
moved to cut the very generous salaries Boyle and his staff had
enjoyed. Miller reduced the annual salary of UMW president
from $50,000, with an automatic per diem of $25, to $35,000,
with no automatic per diem. Mike Trbovich and Harry Patrick,
vice president and secretary-treasurer respectively, cut their
salaries from $40,000 a year plus per diem, to $30,000 with no
per diem. New international staff also took similar cuts. Chip
Yablonski's salary dropped to $35,000 from the $48,000 his
predecessor received, and Rick Bank's pay fell a full 50 percent, from $40,000 to $20,000. When these cuts were added to

reductions of 20 to 40 percent in the earnings of other staffers and minor officials, the UMW estimated it would save $400,000 a year or more than $1,000 a day.[3]

While the new administration found the interim, pro-Miller IEB useful in purging the headquarters of Boyle people, assembling a talented and dedicated staff, and reducing salaries, the election of all district officers remained high on its list of priorities. In line with its campaign promises, the Miller administration moved quickly to provide this opportunity to the membership. On February 15, 1973, the *UMW Journal* announced plans for district elections, including, in most cases, elections for IEB members, to be held in nine districts between May and August of that year.[4] In the following months the international union scheduled elections for seven other districts, so that within a year of the Miller administration's inauguration, the UMW had conducted sixteen district elections. These district elections, in most cases, included races for the top three offices in each district—IEB representative, district president, and district secretary-treasurer—in addition to a number of lesser posts. In all, the 1973 elections filled fifteen IEB slots.

The elections held the key to many of the problems that faced the Miller administration during its first term. The crucial nature of those elections has served to fuel the fire of controversy over the role that Miller and MFD played in the 1973 district elections. That role was essentially one of abstinence and nonintervention.[5]

During its seven-month campaign the highly publicized MFD movement had gained supporters in every district of the UMW. Thousands of rank-and-file miners actively participated and worked in the campaign, forming an informal network of UMW members dedicated to putting Miller and his slate in office. Even though the district elections followed virtually on the heels of the international election, Miller chose not to throw the weight of the movement behind reformist candidates in the districts. Rather than mobilize the campaign apparatus that had sprung up, the MFD leader apparently decided "to let the movement die quickly in an attempt to heal the MFD-Boyle wounds."[6] Harry Patrick, Miller's secretary-treasurer, called the atrophy of MFD "tragic" and said, "Arnold never saw the need to keep it together and he let it die."[7]

Even though MFD at the national level had been all but officially laid to rest, a number of district candidates, like Lou Antal of District 5 and Jack Perry of District 17, ran as MFD or reform candidates and effectively utilized the MFD networks developed during the international election. However, as soon as the district elections concluded, the successful MFD candidates called for the end of the reform organization, much as Miller had. Antal, a long-time reform supporter and victorious MFD candidate for the District 5 (western Pennsylvania) presidency stated, "The need for MFD has ceased to exist and we now must devote our time to rejuvenating the union that we all want to serve and must improve."[8]

Perry, who won the southern West Virginia District 17 president's job under the MFD banner, voiced the same sentiment: "It (MFD) got what we wanted . . . But we are United Mine Workers and not Miners for Democracy."[9]

Many individuals active in the reform movement, both rank-and-filers and candidates for union office, criticized Miller for his attitude toward MFD and the district elections. As one observer of the scene put it, Miller "tried to move ahead with his reform program without establishing a supportive political structure at the district and local levels."[10] Miller's stance, however, probably had little effect on the outcomes of the district elections. In the 1972 Miller-Boyle election, Miller won in ten of the UMW's twenty-two voting districts. In the district elections held in these Miller strongholds, eight of the ten districts elected candidates with a pro-Miller, pro-MFD affiliation. In the eight districts that went for Boyle in 1972 and subsequently held district elections, seven of those districts elected nonreform candidates (either pro-Boyle or anti-Boyle, anti-Miller) over those associated with the reform forces. Of the fourteen individuals appointed by Miller to IEB positions in the early days of his administration, only four won election in their own right in subsequent district elections: Ed Monborne in District 2, John Kelly in District 4, Frank Clements in District 20, and William Savitsky in District 25. Non-MFD candidates, in most cases Boyle supporters, defeated Miller appointees in head-to-head elections in six districts: Districts 14, 19, 23, 29, 30, and 31.[11] While the lack of an organized MFD effort might have contributed to the defeat of these Miller-backed candidates, the strength of the Boyle forces in some districts, even after the election, was probably responsible for the success of the nonreform candidates.

These elections drew the battlelines for the continual skirmishes between Miller and the IEB that plagued his initial term. The results created two intensely partisan factions, separated by a somewhat amorphous buffer zone of less committed and combative individuals. Three IEB members, first appointed by Miller and consequently elected in district elections, constituted the core of Miller allies on the board. These included Monborne of District 2 in western Pennsylvania, Miller's campaign manager in the 1972 election; Kelly of District 4, also in western Pennsylvania; and Savitsky of District 25 in the eastern Pennsylvania anthracite coalfields. A number of men who served in the Boyle administration made up the nucleus of the opposition Miller would face from the IEB. Most notable among these were Lee Roy Patterson of District 23 in western Kentucky, who had served as the appointed president of that district before 1973; Andrew Morris, formerly appointed head of District 31 in northern West Virginia; and Frank Stevenson of District 22 in the western United States, also formerly an appointed president of his district.

The opposition on the IEB acted as a check on the Miller administration's reform program. Despite this resistance, the new leadership continued its efforts to rebuild the UMW. During the first year, the administration channeled much of its energy into major reform programs involving safety and the Welfare and Retirement Funds. Safety was a key issue in the 1972 election campaign, and when the reform candidates took office they made improved safety in the mines a top priority. Moving quickly, the new administration expanded and completely reorganized the UMW's safety division, initiated a training program for union safety personnel at all levels, developed materials to assist safety officials in their jobs,[12] and published regular features in the *UMW Journal* to inform the membership about this vital area.[13]

Table 2   The Reform Movement and the 1973 District Elections

District	1972 Election Results	IEB Election Winner Affiliation	IEB Election Winner	Date of Election
2 Central Penna.	Miller	Miller-MFD	Ed Monborne*	6/73
3 Western Penna.	Boyle	(Merged with District 5 after 1972 Election)		
4 Western Penna.	Miller	Miller-MFD	John Kelly*	6/73
5 Western Penna.	Miller	Miller-MFD	Nick DeVince	5/73
6 Ohio	Miller	Miller-MFD	Karl Kafton	12/72
10 Washington	Boyle	(Merged with District 15 after 1972 Election)		
11 Indiana	Boyle	Nonreform	Robert Edney	10/73
12 Illinois	Miller	Miller-MFD	Gene Mitchell	12/72
14 Iowa, Kansas, Missouri	Boyle	Nonreform	Robert Long†	8/73
15 Colorado, New Mexico	Miller	Nonreform	Nick Halamandaris	3/74
17 Southwest West Virginia	Miller	Miller-MFD	Ivan White	6/73
19 Kentucky, Tennessee	Boyle	Nonreform	Lonnie Brown†	10/73
20 Alabama	Boyle	Miller-MFD	Frank Clements*	9/73
21 Texas, Oklahoma, Arkansas	Boyle	(Position vacant until 1-2/75)		
22 Utah, Wyoming, Arizona	Boyle	Nonreform	Frank Stevenson	12/73
23 Western Kentucky	Boyle	Nonreform	Lee Roy Patterson†	6/73
25 Eastern Penna.	Miller	Miller-MFD	William Savitsky*	6/73
27 Montana	Boyle	(Merged with District 15 after 1973 Election)		
28 Virginia	Miller	Miller-MFD	Elmer Church	11/73
29 Southeast West Virginia	Boyle	Nonreform	Francis Martin†	11/73
30 Eastern Kentucky	Boyle	Nonreform	J.B. Trout†	8/73
31 Northern West Virginia	Miller	Nonreform	Andrew Morris	6/73

Notes: *—Original Miller appointees
†—Candidates defeating Miller appointees in elections
Source: *UMW Journal*

Key reforms in the Welfare and Retirement Funds began as soon as the reformers took office. The Miller administration moved immediately to implement the reorganization of the Funds ordered by the federal courts in their decisions of 1972.[14] The newly elected officers appointed Washington attorney Harry Huge as the union's new trustee, pushed for full-scale revamping of the Funds organization, sought to extend benefits to widows and disabled miners, and tried to expand benefits for those currently eligible for Funds benefits.[15]

Reforms occurred in other important areas of the union. In many of the remote towns and rural areas of the coalfields, the *UMW Journal,* received by all union members, has often been the only national publication of any kind read by miners and their families. Used as an instrument of leadership under Lewis and Boyle, the reform administration opened the publication to the membership. The new *Journal* staff replaced flattering stories about the officers, pages of government regulations, and trivial news stories, comics, and recipes, with a letter-to-the-editor page, a regular "Rank-and-File Speaks" feature, which presented both supportive and critical viewpoints, and relevant articles on safety, health, energy, politics, and union history. The *Journal* had a new function and purpose. It was to act as "an important source of information and expression for the rank-and-file."[16]

In February 1973, one month after taking office, the UMW set up the Field Service Office (FSO) in Charleston, West Virginia. The FSO's purpose was to provide a coalfield office to assist miners and their families with benefits and claims involving black lung, worker's compensation, Welfare and Retirement Funds, and other union or governmental assistance to which they might be entitled. The FSO also acted as a clearinghouse and referral center for other public or community services available to members and their dependents.[17] The reform administration provided another new and innovative service to mining families when it formed the UMW Federal Credit Union. Open only to UMW members, the credit union provided a place where "miners' money could work for miners" and from which miners could obtain otherwise elusive loans.[18]

While Miller and his officers could purge the union of many

of the visible remnants of the Boyle administration, the real dangers presented by a regime such as Boyle's ran deeper than the individuals immediately involved or the salaries they received. Changing the individuals or their salaries, approaching the union's problems with new enthusiasm, or even instituting new programs could not totally eradicate the problems or precedents left to the new officers. Over the years that Lewis and Boyle had ruled the UMW, their abuses of power and methods of retaining control had become institutionalized. They had shaped the structure and law of the union to meet their specifications. If true reform was to occur, more than the highly visible elements of the union had to change. The new administration realized this and early in their first year in office scheduled an international convention for December 3 to 14, 1973.[19] This convention was necessary, not only because it was the sole mechanism through which the union's governing rules and its constitution could be changed, but also because the officers realized that reform must involve the rank and file. Reform by executive decree would have been inconsistent with the basic principles of the movement that had put them in office. The convention provided the perfect opportunity for the membership to play a leading role in the reformation of their union.

Yet, just as the autocratic practices of past administrations had become institutionalized, so had the manner in which the previous leadership manipulated the convention mechanism. As described in Chapter 1, the two Boyle conventions held before the MFD takeover had gone beyond the abuse of the convention process that had occurred under Lewis. In the face of such precedent, it was apparent that broad changes in the convention process itself were necessary.

The introduction to the 1973 UMWA convention proceedings states that "elected on a broadly based movement of reform, Miller, Trbovich, and Patrick quickly found that building new structures meant demolishing old foundations. Nowhere was this razing and rebuilding so evident than at the union's convention."[20] Even though only one officer, Trbovich, had ever attended a UMW convention before, the officers were aware that in order to present a situation where the rank and file could genuinely and effectively reform their union a convention was necessary. "While tempted to enter the convention buttressed by the same props that had been used so successfully by previous administrations,"[21] the new officers decided to base the plan for the convention on democratic premises. Two of these were that "the convention must be democratic (and) it must involve the rank-and-file in substantive policy formulation and give the officers a mandate on the union's direction for the next four years."[22] In order to achieve these goals, the Miller administration initiated reforms in the convention mechanics; some proved effective, some did not.

The first step toward making the convention a valid exercise in union democracy was to make sure that the delegation, as truly as possible, reflected the membership. To this end, the IEB passed a resolution on January 4, 1973, dissolving all bogus locals and permitting only active locals to send delegates.[23] In addition they "abolished the restrictive meeting attendance requirement, which favored entrenched local union officials over rank-and-file dissidents."[24] Thus the officers "encouraged new members to seek delegate credentials" and attempted to shift "the preponderance of representation to the working membership."[25]

Another vital area of reform recognized by the Miller administration was the committee system. The first measure taken to remove the precedents left by Boyle and Lewis concerning committees was to abolish totally the exorbitant stipends that committee members received for their work. Expenses would still be covered, but they would be closely checked. In addition, the reform administration reduced the size of the committees and abolished a number of nonessential standing committees.[26]

Although Miller still retained the powerful privilege of appointing the committee members, he did establish a set of criteria aimed at making the committee a valid and effective organ of the convention. Among his standards of selection were the need to create balance among districts and between retired and active members and, most notably, the need for "a political balance . . . between identified opponents and supporters of the new leadership."[27] Miller successfully balanced the committees logistically, but this in itself would not ensure a balance of opinion. Miller did appoint several declared opponents to committees, but overall it is difficult to determine whether he achieved the principle of political balance since, in many cases, political loyalties during this period were somewhat transient and undefined. It is probably safe to assume that the makeup of the committees probably more or less reflected his personal political philosophy and opinions.

Realizing that the rules by which a convention operates have a tremendous influence on the democratic character of the proceedings, the Rules Committee proposed and won acceptance of several crucial revisions in the convention rules. Introducing these revisions, the committee noted,

> We want to prove and to demonstrate to all concerned that the United Mine Workers is, in fact, a free and democratic organization, and that can only be done if the representatives of the rank-and-file are given every opportunity to be heard today and throughout the sessions.[28]

The rule changes enacted made it more difficult to cut off discussion, allowed for freer debate and expression, and called for minority reports to be presented along with majority reports when committees deadlocked over an issue.[28] The committee made a significant revision when it scrapped a longstanding policy preventing the amending of committee reports by delegates on the floor.[30] This rule change weakened the absolute power the committees previously wielded over the substance of resolutions reaching the floor. To assist the inexperienced officers and delegates in the democratic process, the new administration obtained the services of an experienced parliamentarian from the United Auto Workers Union.[31]

The convention proceedings were anything but dull as the delegates tasted the heady wine of unaccustomed democracy. "The convention seesawed between anarchy and control, as the chair wavered between a free-wheeling, let-everyone-speak approach and more formal parliamentary style."[32] Early in the proceedings, Miller expressed his philosophy of chairing the convention:

> I'm not a lawyer and I'm no super-parliamentarian, but I do believe in democracy, and I have one guiding belief,

and that is if it is fair and democratic and gives the delegates at this convention an opportunity to express themselves, then we will be running a good convention.[33]

To some, especially those who had experienced a Lewis or Boyle convention, the chairman's flexible style and the delegates' aggressive debate on all controversial resolutions were inappropriate. One delegate, Mike Hajduk of Local 6295 in District 4 (Pennsylvania), expressed his irritation to the chair:

You have been trying to conduct this convention in as democratic a way as possible. Democracy is good because it's freedom. I think it is being abused here at this convention, and you are being taken advantage of. That's my personal opinion. I think it is high time that the delegates start heading in one direction, because there seems to be a split here. I think you have been more than tolerant, and I think it is high time we put an end to it.[34]

Undoubtedly Arnold Miller and many delegates were unsure and inexperienced at the 1973 convention. As Miller admitted late in the proceedings, "We are going through a learning process."[35] In retrospect, it seems that if Arnold Miller erred as chairman of the 1973 convention, he erred on the side of openness and expression. If the delegates to that convention erred in their role as representatives of the rank and file, they erred on the side of candor and enthusiasm. At that point in the emerging democracy's experience, these responses seem to have been appropriate and necessary ones.

The proceedings may have been chaotic, but a number of concrete strides were made toward a more democratic union at the convention. Most of these gains came in the form of constitutional amendments. In January 1974, the postconvention *UMW Journal* optimistically proclaimed these reforms in its headlines when it blared, "New Constitution Guarantees Members' Right to Democracy."[36] The *Journal* went on to report,

The UMWA has a new Constitution that expands the membership's democratic rights within the union. It contains provisions to insure fair and honest elections at every level of the UMWA and prevents improper interference or reprisals for support of any candidate. The new Constitution insures full district autonomy and the rank-and-file ratifications of contracts. It also contains trial procedures that allow charges to be brought against members or officers while protecting their rights.[37]

The 1973 convention completely revamped the constitution's election provisions to ensure that the Boyle-Yablonski debacle would never occur again. Between 1926 and 1969 the democratic election process in the UMW had atrophied. Before Yablonski's challenge, few living miners could remember the last time the union's president faced anything more than the formality of reelection. For this reason it was necessary to completely rebuild the election mechanism. Most of the safeguards applied in the government-supervised election of 1972 were incorporated in the revisions. These safeguards included the guarantee that "every member shall have the right to nominate, vote for, and otherwise support the candidate of his choice free from penalty, discipline, improper interference, or reprisal of any kind."[38] It also included the provisions that "no funds belonging to the Union or controlled by an employer shall be used to promote the candidacy of any candidate,"[39] and "no appointed employee or elected officer shall be required to make any contribution or . . . be subsequently dismissed or penalized . . . for having failed to support a particular candidate."[40]

A second step in laying the groundwork for democracy involved formalizing the right of district autonomy, provisionally restored by the district elections held soon after MFD took office. Constitutional amendments, placing tight controls over the international's power to bring a district (or a local) under trusteeship and over the duration of any such action, accomplished this needed reform.[41] Thus, aside from the most unusual circumstances, the constitution guaranteed all districts the right to elect their administrative officers. The convention also restructured the dues allocation provision to ensure that the districts would not be held in economic vassalage.

Because of the vital nature of bargaining, the convention moved quickly to reconstruct the union's collective bargaining process in an attempt to allow greater membership participation and involvement. In order to move away from the "imperial bargaining" of the Lewis-Boyle era, a new procedure for channeling rank-and-file demands and priorities was created.[42]

In addition, a new procedure for rank-and-file ratification of any proposed contract based on a full explanation of all terms and provisions was approved.[43]

In an attempt to further protect the rights of the membership, the constitution written at the 1973 convention included a detailed procedure for the trial of any member or official charged with failing to carry out his union duties, misuse of funds, election fraud, or the violation of another member's democratic rights. The process involved a trial committee made up of union members and was designed to prosecute fairly those charged with violations of union policy or law, while simultaneously protecting the rights of the accused.[44]

Another important step taken at the convention involved the role of the pensioner in union affairs. In order to better represent the interests and concerns of the retired member, the convention created the position of international vice president for pensioner affairs. This action provided full-time representation to this large, yet often neglected segment of the membership.[45]

If effectively enforced, the new constitution and its many reforms could go far in making the transition to union democracy a reality. Paper reforms, however, were not sufficient to rebuild the union, and only time could tell how this new framework would be used. The 1973 convention, while unable to change the regressive tendencies of the previous fifty years overnight, did in any event lay the substantive foundations upon which a more democratic UMW could be built.

The 1973 UMW convention was a watershed in the history of the union. It not only laid the foundation for structural changes that would allow democracy to exist within the union, it revived the actual practice of democracy by the union membership. It was the rank and file, not executive edict or outside influence, that was reforming and rebuilding the union. The open and democratic convention was the means by which this was achieved. Thomas Stark, a rank-and-file miner from Ohio who had attended every UMW convention since the thirties, testified to the progress made in Pittsburgh in 1973 when he told the convention, "I can say as a witness that this has been the most open and democratic convention that I have ever attended."[46]

3 Collective Bargaining Reform and the 1974 Contract

R AZING and rebuilding consumed the reform administration's first year in office. The 1973 convention capped this period by rewriting the UMWA constitution.

Included among the many reforms written into the new constitution by the 1973 convention was a completely revamped collective bargaining procedure. Since the current United Mine Workers–Bituminous Coal Operators' Association contract expired November 12, 1974, making 1974 a bargaining year, the union did not need to wait long to implement its revised bargaining process.

The new procedure differed greatly from the bargaining process employed by John L. Lewis and Tony Boyle and, in itself, constituted a major democratic reform. The process employed during the Lewis and Boyle years had no constitutional basis. Before 1973, no definitive bargaining guidelines existed in the UMWA constitution; in fact, nowhere was specific authorization granted to the president to negotiate on behalf of the membership.[1] As in so many other facets of the union's administration, the leadership simply assumed both the authority for, and the structure of, collective bargaining. The delegates to the 1973 convention succeeded in rectifying this situation and its attendant abuses by delineating in specific constitutional terms the collective bargaining procedures and the authority granted to the president.[2]

The collective bargaining procedures adopted by the convention made up an entirely new article in the UMWA constitution, Article XIX—Negotiations and Strikes. The first section of the article adopted by the delegates created the Bargaining Council to take the place of the National Wage Policy Committee of the Lewis-Boyle era. The Bargaining Council would be "responsible for using all means practicable to determine the desires of the members, both before negotiations begin and as negotiations progress."[3] The Bargaining Council was to serve as a link facilitating rank-and-file involvement in the bargaining process. This group would consist of International Executive Board members and district presidents, all of whom would be union officials elected according to other amendments enacted at the 1973 convention.[4]

Section 2 of this new article made provisions for holding district conferences in each of the union's twenty-one districts before negotiations: "The purpose of the District Conference shall include obtaining suggestions, views, and recommendations reflecting the desires of the members as to what demands should be made and what priorities should be set in the negotiations."[5] The conferences provided a vehicle by which the rank and file could directly make their views known to those conducting negotiations.

Section 3 of Article XIX delegated authority to the president of the UMW to conduct negotiations on behalf of the membership.[6] This was part of the movement to restrict the powers of the president to certain areas, a move necessitated by the assumption of very broad powers by previous UMW presidents.

The next section of the article, Section 4, spelled out the duties of the Bargaining Council created in Section 1:

> The Bargaining Council shall decide the demands to be made in negotiations and the policies and priorities to be followed in negotiations . . . When the Bargaining Council

recommends the adoption of a proposed agreement, it shall be submitted to a ratification vote. . . .[7]

Ultimately, somebody must decide what demands, policies, and priorities are going to guide negotiations. The bargaining process conceived at the 1973 convention conferred this responsibility on the Bargaining Council. The effort to ensure maximum rank-and-file involvement in the formulation of demands and priorities lies in the recommendations of the district conferences, the collective bargaining recommendations of the previous UMW convention, and the provision that all of the council members would be elected by the membership. While the recommendations of conferences and conventions would not be binding on the Bargaining Council, the need for contract ratification by the membership, as required in Section 7 of Article XIX, would ensure that an effort would be made to pursue the wishes of the rank and file. In addition, this section provided that the council must approve any agreement before it is submitted to the ratification process.[8]

Section 7 states:

> Ratification votes shall be held in each Local Union which has members covered by the agreement and shall be conducted only after opportunity for full explanation of the proposed agreement and full opportunity for discussion and debate . . . . No agreement shall be effective until it has been approved by a majority vote of all the valid ballots cast by participating members.[9]

The passage of this provision fulfilled one of the promises fundamental to the Miners for Democracy campaign by establishing rank-and-file ratification of all contracts. Section 7 also laid down the mechanisms of the ratification process and ensured its validity as a democratic exercise by providing for secret ballots in convenient places.[10]

The collective bargaining procedure within the UMW that evolved out of the Miners for Democracy reform movement and the 1973 UMW convention is, on paper, a truly democratic process involving the rank and file from top to bottom. The process begins at the local union where members elect delegates to district conferences on collective bargaining and to the national UMW convention. Delegates representing every local take the opinions of their constituents to conferences and conventions where, in consultation with other delegates, a consensus is arrived at. The recommendations of these bodies are then presented to a Bargaining Council, which is itself composed of elected representatives. The council considers the recommendations from the lower bodies and attempts to arrive at a consensus that is representative of the membership.

The negotiating team, led by the president of the union, takes Bargaining Council recommendations to the bargaining table. When a tentative agreement is reached it is presented to the Bargaining Council, which either sends it back to negotiations or passes it to the membership for ratification. In most cases the proposal is explained to the delegates of the district conferences, who in turn take the contract back to their respective locals for explanation, debate, and eventually a vote. If the contract is approved, the union officers may sign it. If it is not approved, the negotiating team must continue to negotiate, seeking improvement in the rejected contract.[11]

The revamped bargaining process, passed in 1973, went a step further in involving the UMW convention in collective bargaining by formalizing the delegation's previously customary duty to review and recommend bargaining priorities for upcoming negotiations. The 1973 convention considered 70 recommendations[12] distilled by the Collective Bargaining Committee from more than 1,350 resolutions.[13] Acting on these recommendations, the delegation established fringe benefits as its top bargaining priority. Sick pay, common to many other industries but completely absent in the coal industry, headed the list. Cost-of-living adjustments (COLAs) designed to keep miners' wages on par with inflation; graduated vacations, allowing more vacation time for miners with greater seniority; and increased holidays were also high on the delegates' list of priorities. "Substantial wage increases to catch up with the cost of living" and safety issues were among the other recommendations made by the convention to the union's negotiators.[14]

While theoretically an effective democratic procedure in which bargaining begins and ends with the membership, the new process passed in 1973 would not be tested until the fol-

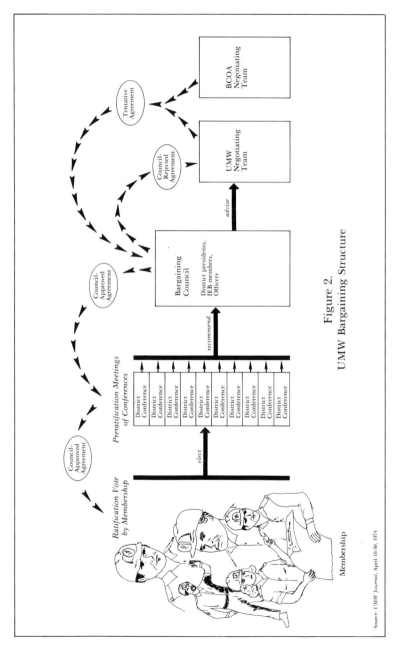

Figure 2.
UMW Bargaining Structure

Source: *UMW Journal*, April 16-30, 1974

lowing year. Its implementation in 1974 would achieve mixed results.

The participation of the membership of any organization in a democratic decision-making process is based on the assumption that the members have the requisite knowledge and information to consider alternatives and make choices based on their analysis of these alternatives. Beyond this, the membership must have an understanding of the procedure itself and their responsibilities within this procedure. Long before most of the mechanisms of the bargaining procedure started to function, the UMW began to supply the members with the information necessary to participate in the democratic process.

The *United Mine Workers Journal,* a semimonthly publication, served as the main instrument through which the union carried out this education program. Beginning in early 1974, long before contract talks opened on September 3, the *UMW Journal* devoted many of its pages to articles informing the membership of the new contract procedures, the conditions of the coal industry, the state of the United States economy, and the circumstances of the energy crisis. Later, the *Journal* kept the membership informed of important developments during negotiations, including publication in full of the contract demands presented to the operators and the complete text of the proposed contract upon which the membership would vote.[15]

One illustration comparing the openness of the 1974 negotiations and the effort made to inform the rank and file with the clandestine nature of negotiations under the Boyle administration was the number of pages devoted to contract-related topics in the *UMW Journal.* Before, during, and after the 1964 contract talks, the *Journal* ran 13 pages containing contract-related articles. The 1968 negotiations, again, merited only 13 pages of contract stories over a three-month period. In 1971, due to the occurrence of a strike and the tenuous political position of the Boyle administration at the time, the *Journal* increased its coverage of negotiations to 48 pages. Under Miller in 1974, the *Journal* devoted 105 pages to negotiations or contract-related stories over a nine-month period—more than eight times the information supplied under Boyle in 1964 and 1968 and over twice the amount published in 1971. The quality of coverage under Miller also improved significantly as detailed explanations and extensive background information supplemented the basic facts and bare text that had often constituted coverage during the Boyle years. Clearly, an informed rank and file was a much higher priority during the 1974 UMW collective bargaining process.[16]

Entering negotiations in 1974 the UMW's bargaining power was probably as great as it had been at any time in more than twenty-five years. With the nation still reeling from the oil shortage of the early seventies, coal was again emerging as an important industry. Company profits had skyrocketed over the previous few years and looked even more promising in 1974. In the first half of 1974 alone, the Pittston Company reported profits of $39,054,000, an 868 percent increase over the previous year's first half.[17] In addition, coal stockpiles were significantly lower than during the 1971 talks, due, in part, to a week-long "memorial period" work stoppage honoring victims of mining disasters and coal company violence called by Miller a few weeks before the start of negotiations.[18]

The first district conference on collective bargaining, as provided for under the 1973 constitution, was held on May 7, 1974, and included delegates from Districts 2, 4, and 5 in western and central Pennsylvania. In opening the meeting, Lou Antal, president of District 5, noted, "This is an historic occasion for the United Mine Workers. For the first time ever, the leadership is asking the rank-and-file what they want, instead of telling them what they are going to get."[19] The district bargaining conferences, like the 1973 international convention, presented a new opportunity for the membership to become involved in the union's decision-making process. Through discussions of the union's new bargaining process, the state of the coal industry, and the United States economy, and the more practical aspects of union democracy, the conferences served as learning experiences in the procedural and substantive aspects of collective bargaining. The *UMW Journal* described the first conference:

> The day-long gathering was a first for the union and, like a ship on its shakedown cruise, it suffered through

occasional stormy moments as delegates got down to the hard realities of collective bargaining. By late afternoon, virtually every man had a chance to outline the contract priorities and proposals given him by his local.[20]

In all, the UMW scheduled thirteen conferences in the areas of the country where coal was mined under the Bituminous Coal Operators' Association (BCOA) agreement. Members of the union's bargaining council attended each of the conferences and, on completion of the process, drew up a series of position papers based on the views expressed in the districts. These position papers, combined with the collective bargaining recommendations of the 1973 convention, articulated the rank and file's priorities for the 1974 contract and served as the basis for the union's initial positions in negotiations.[21]

On September 3, 1974, the UMW negotiating team presented the BCOA with its initial contract demands, which included more than two hundred proposals. The list was headed by demands for improved fringe benefits, wage and cost-of-living increases, improved health and safety provisions, and a substantial royalty increase for the UMW Welfare and Retirement Funds.[22] In rejecting virtually all of the UMW's initial proposals on September 18, the BCOA made clear its desire for only "minor alterations" in the 1971 agreement. They rejected the "start from scratch" approach of the union.[23] This inauspicious beginning to negotiations notified all concerned that the short-and-sweet style of bargaining that had been the rule in the industry since 1950 was about to change.

The BCOA held its hard line on noneconomic issues and on October 10 the UMW Bargaining Council unanimously rejected management's "final" offer in this area.[24] Although bargaining did continue on noneconomic issues, progress was slow. The parties did not even discuss economic issues until the last few days of October. Due to the lengthy ratification process, an effective strike deadline fell ten days in advance of the November 12 contract expiration date, and the union, industry, and government girded for a nationwide bituminous coal strike.

The November 12 deadline came and "soft-coal mines went down all over America as more than 120,000 UMW members walked off the job, honoring a long tradition of 'No contract-no work.'"[25] Aided by around-the-clock bargaining, the parties reached a tentative agreement on November 13. The new bargaining process required that any tentative agreement first be approved by the Bargaining Council before the membership ratification procedure could be set in motion. On November 20, the Bargaining Council rejected the new agreement and instructed the negotiating team to seek additional improvements at the bargaining table.[26] The reasons for this initial rejection were complex. Union politics, however, certainly played a role. The rift that developed over the proposed contract between Miller and the middle-level officers who made up the council was to become a fact of life in the UMW.

Six days later, on November 26, the negotiating team laid a revised agreement on the table for Bargaining Council approval. The second proposed contract had an additional 1 percent increase in wages and benefits over a three-year period, a total increase of from 53 percent in the initial agreement to 54 percent in the new proposal.[27] The council first rejected this revised proposal, but later the same day approved it by a vote of twenty-two to fifteen.[28]

Rank-and-file ratification was a new process to the union and to the members, so it was expected that problems would arise when the administration set the procedure into motion. District conferences reconvened on Saturday, November 30, four days after the contract had been approved by the Bargaining Council. In these conferences, UMW officers and staff explained the proposed agreement to the assembled local union representatives. These local representatives, in turn, went back to their local unions to explain the contract to the entire membership. In the meantime, the *UMW Journal* rushed a special issue to the printer containing a detailed explanation and the full text of the agreement. Almost every member had a copy in hand before voting on ratification.[29]

Local unions held meetings between December 1 and 4 for the purpose of conducting contract discussions and ratification votes. The turnout for these meetings was relatively low; only 65 percent of those eligible to vote actually did. A number of diverse factors contributed to this light response, including confusion over the terms of the agreement, confusion over the ratification process itself, an eastern snowstorm, and the opening of deer season in Pennsylvania.[30]

The final count listed 44,754 votes in favor of ratification and 34,741 opposed, a 56 percent to 44 percent vote in favor of the contract.[31] Since just 44,754 out of the 121,536 miners covered by the contract voted for ratification, only slightly more than 36 percent had voted to approve it. The 1976 officers' report analyzed the vote:

> Although technically this more than met the requirements for adoption of the new contract, it also spelled trouble ahead—for the simple reason that more than half the people who would work under the new contract either hadn't voted at all or had voted against it, for one reason or another.[32]

On December 5, 1974, Arnold Miller signed the agreement marking the end of a twenty-four day nationwide soft coal strike. The start-from-scratch approach of the UMW largely succeeded as the contract that emerged made great advances over those of past years. Among the gains won by the UMW in 1974 were a week of paid sick leave each year plus a sickness and accident benefit plan; pension increases of as much as $250 a month for currently retired miners; a wage package that with cost-of-living allowance to protect against inflation, could amount to more than 37 percent over three years; the guaranteed right of an individual to withdraw from a hazardous area; a streamlined grievance procedure with mandatory time limits as well as an arbitration review process; and an increase in the number of total paid days off from twenty to thirty.[33] The union also negotiated a number of other improvements in the areas of safety training and inspection, job bidding, helpers on dangerous equipment, and royalty payments.[34]

There were some problems with the 1974 contract, including the inequities created between the pension plan for miners retiring after 1976 and the less generous plan for those retiring earlier, difficult contract language, and the failure to obtain a right-to-strike provision. Overall, however, the new contract represented a victory for the union. The 64 percent increased cost to the industry made it "the second largest increase ever won by a union—exceeded only by the Alaska oil pipeline workers."[35] The wage gains raised the coal miner's average daily earnings to $54.39,[36] slightly higher than those of his counterpart in auto and steel, and well above the average manufacturing wage.[37] The contract was truly a bench mark for the UMW and its members.

Although Arnold Miller, as chief negotiator for the union, had ultimate responsibility for negotiations, at least an equal amount of credit for the vastly improved contract belonged to sources other than the union leadership. The new bargaining process, providing for greatly increased membership involvement, allowed union members to determine to a large extent the nature and priority of contract demands. In addition, the final decision on whether to accept the BCOA offer resided not with Miller or the Bargaining Council but with the rank and file. In terms of the technical aspect of negotiations and the day-to-day bargaining, Miller benefited greatly from the preparation, research, and advice of a staff of young, highly capable aides, including Chip Yablonski, UMW general counsel; Rick Bank, attorney and executive assistant to the president; and Tom Bethell, director, and Tom Woodruff, economist, in the UMW research department.[38]

Before 1972, the trend in the UMW had been toward increasingly centralized control over all aspects of the union in the top echelons of the leadership. Both Lewis and Boyle had based the union's collective bargaining procedures on this principle of centralized decision-making, while granting the union's members little, if any, voice in this most fundamental process. The Miller administration made the restructuring of the union's bargaining process to allow more rank-and-file input a high priority. It is significant that the reforms in the bargaining process occurred in the democratic forum of the 1973 convention. Rank-and-file delegates to the convention, not executive edict, changed the process. The bargaining procedure that evolved applied the principles of democracy to ensure membership participation in all phases of the negotiations process.

Churchill once said that "democracy is the worst possible system of government. Except for all the others."[39] The democratic

55

bargaining process, first employed in 1974, had its problems. Nonetheless, that year the UMW negotiated its best contract while allowing extensive rank-and-file input, including final approval by the membership, into the process. Given the fundamental importance of collective bargaining to any labor organization, the reform of the UMW's bargaining process and the 1974 agreement that evolved from this process stand as one of the Miller administration's greatest accomplishments.

4   Internal Strife

THE transition from corrupt kingdom to rank-and-file union was difficult for the United Mine Workers. Without a democratic heritage among the membership and without trained and proven leaders to guide it, the union in 1972 found itself in uncharted territory. Turmoil has remained a constant companion of union democracy in the UMW ever since. The years following the contract negotiations of 1974 were particularly turbulent. The difficulties that plagued the union between 1974 and the end of Miller's first term were centered in two distinct but related areas, political factionalism and wildcat strikes.

The reform administration's difficulties in the political arena stemmed mainly from opposition on the International Executive Board. Ironically, this opposition had its roots in the series of district elections made possible by the new leadership's approach to union government. These elections drew the battle lines for skirmishes that occurred between Miller and the IEB throughout the next four years. The core of Miller's support on the board came from three men first appointed to the IEB by Miller and then elected in their own right: Ed Monborne of District 2, John Kelly of District 4, and William Savitsky of District 25. The leaders of the opposition faction were Lee Roy Patterson of District 23 and Andrew Morris of District 31. Others who consistently opposed the administration included Robert Long of District 14, Nick Halamandaris of District 15, Lonnie Brown of District 19, Donald Lawley of District 21, Francis Martin of District 29, and J. B. Trout of District 30.

Although many of the remaining ten IEB members leaned strongly one way or the other, the whirlwind of union politics prevented these buffer members from becoming firmly committed to any one political side. A split also occurred among the three reform leaders in the third year of their first term, when Vice President Mike Trbovich defected to the anti-Miller faction of the IEB.[1] Secretary-Treasurer Harry Patrick stood firmly behind Miller until the 1977 elections.

The first outward sign of trouble appeared shortly after the 1973 convention. That convention passed a resolution that authorized the UMW president to seek a site in the coalfields for the international headquarters, then located in Washington, D.C.[2] This was a Miners for Democracy campaign promise and a high priority of the new administration. The choice of a new location, however, was subject to the approval of the IEB. After reviewing many possible locations, Miller selected a sixty-four acre site at Teays Valley in southern West Virginia.[3] Despite Miller's endorsement, on three separate occasions in February and March 1974 a majority of the IEB refused to approve the Teays Valley proposal.[4] The reason given for this decision was that some members had not had an opportunity to examine the site. In addition, some members of the IEB who had seen the site described it as "swampland." Though mandated by the 1973 convention, the issue, after a third vote, reached an impasse that would not be resolved during Miller's years in office.[5] The setback was the new president's first showdown with the opposition on the board.

During the remainder of 1974 the UMW concentrated its efforts on contract negotiations. In the Bargaining Council, the body through which IEB members as well as district presidents participated in negotiations, Miller and his IEB opponents again locked horns. After three months of bargaining, with a nationwide bituminous coal strike already in progress, the council rejected the tentative agreement Miller had presented to them on November 13, 1974. After ten more days of bargaining, a majority on the council first voted to reject, then grudgingly approved the contract. The explanations for the council's obstinance ranged from political revenge to genuine concern that the contract should be strengthened.[6] Whatever the case, it had become clear that there were members of the IEB, if not a substantial number of members, who opposed Miller even on the most crucial issues.

Within a month, by January 1975, the fire that had been smoldering under the surface burst into the open. The fuel for the fire was Miller's staff, a group of young, capable nonminers who had manned Miller's 1972 campaign and moved into jobs at the UMW's Washington, D.C., headquarters after his election victory. The controversy was significant, because it was "the first concerted, intra-union attack that his political opponents . . . (had) been willing to publicly acknowledge."[7] The leader of the opposition that surfaced over the staff issue was Lee Roy Patterson, IEB member from District 23 and former Boyle supporter. Patterson, who allegedly "described members of the staff at closed union meetings as 'house reds' and as 'radicals,'" publicly stated that it was the number and ideology of Miller's staff that concerned him.[8] Although Patterson was the only IEB member to criticize the staff publicly, he stated that other board members would join him in a move to force Miller to defend his aides and justify their positions.[9]

The showdown over the staff took place at the February 11, 1975, IEB meeting in Washington, D.C. The *New York Times* reported that Miller confronted Patterson with a demand to substantiate his allegations or, as a union source stated, to "put up or shut up."[10] Patterson was apparently unable to produce any evidence. In addition, the board passed a resolution concerning staff functions, which many interpreted as a show of support for Miller and his staff.[11]

Miller won the battle, but the war had just begun. The staff remained a source of controversy, and Patterson, with a solid faction of board members, continued to oppose the Miller administration in all phases of the union's operations. The dispute over staff and the increasingly combative atmosphere in which union affairs were conducted was undoubtedly a factor in the resignation of some of the key union staff that followed later in the year. Among the first to leave were Chip Yablonski and Dan Edelman of the legal staff, Ed James, presidential assistant, and Don Stillman, editor of the *UMW Journal*.[12]

The infighting reached its most intense level in late October

1975. Within a matter of weeks, Vice President Mike Trbovich openly broke with Miller, led a faction of IEB members in calling for a Department of Labor investigation of UMW financial records, and allegedly masterminded a move by the IEB to oust Miller from office. Trbovich, an early leader of MFD and a leading contender for the MFD presidential nomination, had gracefully accepted the number two position on the slate.[13] During the course of the administration, however, he and Miller had clashed over numerous issues. The rift apparently widened, and by late October 1975, Trbovich had become a leader of the anti-Miller faction on the IEB.[14]

On October 31, Trbovich and other IEB dissidents, in a letter to Department of Labor officials, charged Miller and Secretary-Treasurer Harry Patrick with misspending and overspending union funds and asked that a government audit be conducted.[15] Later that day the board accepted, by a 14-to-5 vote, an otherwise routine report by Vice President for Pensioner Affairs George Vranesh that included a recommendation to call a special UMW convention to remove Miller from office. Although the vote was unconstitutional because the UMW constitution requires a membership petition for officer recall, the move dramatically revealed the depth of the anti-Miller split in the union's high governing body.[16] As expected, such staunch Miller foes as Lee Roy Patterson and Andrew Morris supported the motion. A number of former Miller supporters and appointees also voted in favor of the move, including Karl Kafton, Ivan White, and Frank Clements. Trbovich abstained in the balloting.

The actions of Trbovich and the board met with an angry response in many parts of the coalfields. Many miners resented the IEB's attempt to remove an officer duly elected by the rank and file. In at least one district, miners called for the resignation of their IEB member who had voted to remove Miller.[17] In an attempt to strengthen his power base, Miller began a campaign to inform the rank and file of the board's actions. He also offered to make peace with his vice president and the IEB majority "in order to get on with the business of running this union."[18]

The split that occurred in October and November 1975 was deep-rooted and would prove long-term. The continual chal-

Table 3   International Executive Board Vote on Miller
                Ouster

In Favor of Removal	Opposed	Abstained	Absent
Karl Kafton, Dist. 6	Ed Monborne, Dist. 2	Mike Trbovich, V.P.	FrankStevenson, Dist. 22
Robert Edney, Dist. 11	John Kelly, Dist. 4	Nick DeVince, Dist. 5	Allen Foley, Dist. 26
Gene Mitchell, Dist. 12	Stanley Grocutt, Dist. 18		
Robert Long, Dist. 14	William Savitsky, Dist. 25		
Nick Halamandaris, Dist. 15	Arnold Miller, President		
Ivan White, Dist. 17	Harry Patrick, Sec.-Treas.		
Lonnie Brown, Dist. 19			
Frank Clements, Dist. 20			
Donald Lawley, Dist. 21			
Lee Roy Patterson, Dist. 23			
Arvil Sykes, Dist. 28			
Francis Martin, Dist. 29			
J. B. Trout, Dist. 30			
Andrew Morris, Dist. 31			

lenges that this active opposition group presented to Miller's authority caused him to use extreme measures in dealing with the IEB opposition. On November 26, 1975, Miller suspended District 6 IEB member Karl Kafton, once a staunch Miller-MFD supporter, for direct refusal of an assignment. The IEB lifted the suspension in December.[19] The following January, Miller assigned Lee Roy Patterson to visit a mine in Usibelli, Alaska. Patterson refused, and Miller suspended him for a short time.[20] On April 28, 1976, Miller suspended Vice President Trbovich for thirty days without pay for "refusing a presidential directive to head an International organizing commission in the West."[21] Although the IEB reinstated Trbovich with full back pay on May 19, the insubordination incident marked the end of any meaningful function for Trbovich within Miller's administration.[22] Trbovich was left with little more than a title and ceremonial functions.

The Miller-IEB fight permeated all aspects of the union's operations, a situation that proved detrimental to the best interests of the rank and file. International officers, staff, and IEB members devoted much of their time to attacking and defending one another, and eventually work at the international headquarters slowed to a crawl. Politics hindered organizing, health and safety programs, and contract administration, as staff in these crucial areas were constantly shuffled or caught in the web of factionalism. At one point the IEB voted to severely cut Miller's 1976 budget proposals, a move that would have drastically reduced services provided by the union to the membership. These cuts included a one-third cut in organizing and an 80 percent cut in the Coal Miner's Political Action Committee (COMPAC), the union's political arm, both functions vitally important to the union's existence.[23] Although the IEB later rescinded the cuts, the board's actions left unanswered the question of what had a higher priority within the UMW, union politics or union administration. With factionalism rife in the UMW by the spring and summer of 1976, internal politics loomed as a threat to the future progress of Miller's reform program.

The period from the 1974 contract negotiations through the summer of 1976 was a time of great turmoil in the high reaches of the union. It was also a time of great turmoil at the membership level as wildcat strikes flared up, at first sporadically, but later intensely, all over the coalfields. The geneses of these two problems were closely related.

The movement to democratize the UMW in 1972 brought about a redistribution of power and control aimed at shifting ultimate authority to the membership of the union. The newly won participation in contracts, elections, and other phases of union activity went a long way toward accomplishing this goal as decision making increasingly rested with the rank and file. The redistribution changed the nature of the IEB as it began to act independently and autonomously. The heady sense of freedom that accompanied this democracy undoubtedly played a large role in the problem of wildcat, or unauthorized, strikes that increasingly plagued the Miller administration after 1974.

The incidence of wildcat strikes in the coal industry increased dramatically after the Miller administration took office in 1972. The situation became particularly critical after 1974.[24] Wildcat strikes, however, were not new to the coal industry. Relations between the coal operators and miners have historically been among the most conflictual of any industry. From the coal operator–conceived frame-up and hanging of ten miners in the Molly Maguire affair of the 1870s, to the killing of twenty men, women, and children by the hired gunmen of the Rockefeller-owned Colorado Fuel and Iron Company in 1914, through the violence of the West Virginia and Harlan County, Kentucky, coal mine wars of the twenties and thirties, the coal industry has been the scene of some of the bloodiest, most violent confrontations in the history of American labor.[25] Wildcat strikes have been a part of this conflict. One observer of the wildcat phenomenon in the coal industry has written,

> Miners have a long tradition of taking direct action when they believe an employer has violated the contract, when they have reason to believe that one of their fellows has been wronged, or even to protest political decisions which they feel may affect them adversely. They exhibit high levels of solidarity in such actions and a few disgruntled miners can shut down an entire colliery by walking out.[26]

The picket line is a part of this tradition and is sacred to the coal miner. Miners have added an eleventh commandment to the original ten—"Thou shalt never cross a picket line, anytime, anywhere."[27]

The history of the industry and the union, including the long, bitter fight to win the wages, benefits, and working conditions miners currently enjoy, is one reason for miners' militance and solidarity. Generations of families have followed each other into the mines and have passed down like religion the lesson that coal miners must fight for everything they want.

The nature of the work creates a "feeling of collective responsibility; because mines are so hazardous and the men work in teams, they must rely on each other."[28] In addition, the heritage of rugged independence among the people of rural Appalachia, who make up a large proportion of the work force in the coal mines, has contributed to the tendency to take direct action. Reinforcing the solidarity built at the workplace is the tendency, now changing, of miners and their families to live in close communities.[29]

This militance is not limited to American coal miners. In a study done in the early 1950s, Clark Kerr and Abraham Siegal found that, for basically the same reasons, the inclination to strike is an international characteristic of coal miners. They discovered that in a significant number of countries, coal miners have a high propensity to strike relative to other industrial workers. Similar social and work situations among the coalfields of different countries account for much of the similarity.[30]

The wildcat or unauthorized strike has always been a rank-and-file tactic looked on with disdain by those who negotiate the labor agreement, including the top union officials. As early as 1924, the UMW voiced its disapproval of these actions and established its role as a protector of the bargaining agreement. At that time the leadership wrote a provision into a contract with the northern West Virginia coal operators that stated,

> The United Mine Workers of America recognize that the very fundamental upon which collective bargaining is founded is the strict observance of the wage agreement by both parties to this contract. Local strikes cannot and will not be tolerated.[31]

The penalty for engaging in a local work stoppage, as agreed to by the union's negotiators in this agreement, was a fine of two dollars a day per man.[32]

Under John L. Lewis's scheme of union administration all policies and actions emanated from international headquarters. Yet even during Lewis's day, wildcats were a problem. In 1953, for example, the bituminous coal industry experienced 392 strikes, only a handful of which were union-sanctioned.[33] As in all other phases of union activity, Lewis's method of dealing with this problem was authoritarian. Often his directive sufficed to get the miners back to work, as occurred in a fifteen-day strike of 270,000 workers in 1952.[34] Lewis's political clout within the union was immense, and this weapon could be brought to bear on a key local or district official. If subtle techniques were ineffective, Lewis wielded the cudgel of constitutional authority that enabled him to discipline insurgents with fines and other penalties, as in the 1924 agreement. Through 1947, the two-dollar-a-day fine could be levied against strikers covered under the northern West Virginia agreement. In 1951, Lewis's International Executive Board "established a penalty on local unions for wildcat strikes, ranging from one hundred to five hundred dollars for each 'offense.' "[35] For the most part, however, the respect Lewis commanded and his leadership skills enabled him to deal with this problem and keep it from becoming too severe.

Tony Boyle was less successful in dealing with wildcat strikes than Lewis. Beginning in 1964 a steady increase in the number of local, unauthorized strikes occurred in the coalfields, with wildcats rising from 111 in 1964 to 500 in 1970.[36] In an attempt to deal with this problem, the international union instituted a five-dollar-a-day-per-man fine for wildcat activity that the coal companies collected for the union through the checkoff procedure. This procedure fell into disuse as many companies refused to comply. Later, the industry and the union got together and used a Christmas bonus system to discourage wildcat strikes. At that time miners received a $120 Christmas bonus, but for each month in which strikes occurred during the year, the bonus fell by ten dollars.[37] The measures used by Boyle were generally ineffective. The number of wildcats continued to rise throughout his term in office.

In 1970, something happened that made wildcat strikes an even greater problem for the union. That year the Supreme Court ruled in *Boys Market* v. *Retail Clerks Association* that "a union contract which includes a grievance procedure with binding arbitration in effect bars any strike during the life of the contract."[38] Recent UMW contracts had protected the right to strike; in fact, since 1947 no UMW contract had contained an explicit no-strike pledge. The Supreme Court's rulings, however, recognized an implied no-strike pledge as the quid pro quo for the contract's arbitration clause. The effect was to render any strike between contracts automatically illegal, with the operators having the power to seek and obtain court injunctions to enjoin the strike. To ignore the injunctions subjected miners to contempt of court charges with possible jail terms and stiff fines to follow.[39] Needless to say, this was a tremendous aid to the coal operators who rushed to the courts when strikes occurred. Federal judges obliged just as quickly, the result being that the number of strikes ended under court order rose from "one or two in 1970 to 111 in 1974."[40] This trend continued, with one hundred injunctions being granted from October 1975 to October 1976 in southern West Virginia alone. Wildcat strikes also continued to rise, from 493 to 983 over the same twelve-month span.[41]

Given the heritage of the wildcat strike in the UMW, the heavy-handed efforts of past administrations to hold down walkouts, and a consistent labor relations policy of the industry that miners perceived as aggressive and uncooperative, it is not surprising that the reform administration faced a serious rise in wildcat strike activity. A democratic reform administration could not deal in an authoritarian manner with such rank-and-file actions. Thus, after dropping in 1972, the number of walkouts in the coalfields rose steadily through 1977. The number of man-days lost due to wildcat strikes nearly doubled during the second year of Miller's administration, rising from 529,200 in 1973 to 1,023,800 in 1974. Man-days continued to be lost in greater numbers as the figures rose to 1,417,400 in 1975 and to 1,950,300 in 1976.[42] Thus between the first year of Miller's term and the fourth, the coal industry suffered an increase in man-days lost due to wildcat strikes of approximately 270 percent. In addition, the number of work stoppages in coal reached an all-time high in 1976 of 2,787.[43]

The repercussions of this surge in strike activity affected both the industry and the coal miner. In 1976, the coal industry reported a loss of 20,477,300 tons of potential coal production, 13,434,300 tons more than was reported lost in 1973. Beginning in 1973, tonnage reported lost steadily increased to its high in 1976, and the industry claimed a great loss in profit

Table 4   Wildcat Strike Losses, 1973–76

Years	Man-Days Lost	Payroll Losses	Tonnage Losses	Trust Funds Losses
1973	529,200	$26,298,400	7,043,000	$4,817,400
1974	1,023,800	53,819,000	11,686,700	10,509,500
1975	1,417,400	78,752,200	15,826,000	22,153,200
1976	1,950,300	109,897,900	20,477,300	37,666,300
Total	4,920,700	$268,767,500	55,033,000	$75,146,400

Source: BCOA Research Department

to the coal companies. But not only the industry was hurt by the rash of wildcats. From the time Miller took office in 1972 the amount of wages lost by miners due to strikes rose drastically from $21,783,100 in 1972 to $109,897,900 in 1976, a 400 percent increase.[44] It has been estimated that from the signing of the 1974 agreement to September 1976, the striking miner lost, on average, between $1,500 and $3,500 in wages.[45] In addition to pay lost, wildcat strikes also reportedly cost the miners' Welfare and Retirement Funds more than $88 million since Miller's term had begun in December 1972.[46] Since royalties paid on each ton of coal mined generated the Funds' income, a strike stopping production also halted the payment of royalties to the Funds. This situation put the Funds in a precarious financial situation and forced a decrease in the services provided for miners and their families. For the first time in the thirty-year history of the Funds, the Funds' beneficiaries, beginning July 1, 1977, were forced to pay a share of their hospital and doctor bills.[47]

The reasons for walkouts in coal have always been as diverse and varied as the problems that daily confront the coal miner. A study done at West Virginia University concluded that the issue accounting for the greatest number of work stoppages between 1953 and 1970 in the Appalachia coal industry was working conditions, with wages and benefits being the second most frequent cause of wildcat strikes.[48] While these issues were undoubtedly important in many of the strikes occurring after 1973, an increasingly significant number of large wildcats have centered around issues other than working conditions and wages. Quite a number of strikes during Miller's first term had as their principal cause issues completely outside the formal labor-management relationship. Some of these strikes have been aimed at various levels of government, while some have been aimed primarily at the international union itself. Wildcat strikes, however, did not emerge in a consistent pattern of protest or opposition to the administration. Miller remained fairly popular in West Virginia and Pennsylvania, the loci of the strike problem.

Specific issues were uniformly the cause of the wildcats and ran the gamut of social, political, and international issues. This was particularly the case in 1974. One of the large walkouts that ended in a victory of sorts for the miners was directed at the gasoline rationing policies of West Virginia governor Arch Moore. Miners, who often have to drive long distances to portals, protested Moore's policy barring motorists from buying gasoline if their tank was one-quarter full. The strike began on February 25, idling twenty-seven thousand miners in southern West Virginia, and ended two and one-half weeks later when Moore suspended the gas restriction.[49] In September, another issue completely outside the realm of labor-management relations was responsible for the shutdown of numerous mines in the same part of West Virginia. This time the issue was the use in the Kanawha County schools of controversial textbooks alleged to be trashy and godless in the eyes of the fundamentalist Christian community in and around Charleston. Picketing of the schools by miners and miners' wives spread to coal mines in Kanawha and nearby Boone, Fayette, and Raleigh Counties and idled at least five thousand miners over a ten-day period.[50]

A third strike also transcended the normal bounds of labor relations in its attempts to influence the coal purchasing policies of a southern power conglomerate. Eight thousand miners in Alabama walked off their jobs for a day to protest the Southern Company's purchase of 2.5 million tons of South African coal. The miners were backed by Miller, who accused the company of "subsidizing South African conscript labor at the expense of American miners who will lose jobs to blacks in South Africa working under slave labor conditions."[51]

Miller, generally, however, took no public stands on the wildcat situation in the early years of his administration. Since a great many of the strikes in 1974 were not traditional union-management confrontations, Miller was put in an unusual leadership position. Although not the target in many of the larger strikes, the operators were always the victims and thus, with the court's help, exerted pressure on Miller to get the miners back to work. This was a difficult role for a rank-and-file miner in office for less than two years. Miller seemingly did not feel comfortable ordering miners back to work. So, for the most part, he assumed a generally passive role and exerted little leadership during this period.

After the December 1974 settlement with the BCOA, the wildcat situation intensified. In 1975, the number of wildcat strikes rose to 1,139 from 996 in 1974 and cost 1,417,400 lost man-days.[52] As early as February 1975, five thousand miners closed thirty-three mines in southern West Virginia. The strike eventually escalated to include more than eleven thousand miners in West Virginia, Virginia, and Ohio. The real significance of this strike was that it was a protest solely against the international union. The major bone of contention on the miners' part was the union's delay in distributing copies of the new 1974 agreement. But, as in so many wildcats, secondary issues arose, including dissatisfaction on the part of some miners with the terms of the 1974 contract settlement, particularly the absence of a formal right-to-strike clause. After twenty-three days all the strikers returned to work. Copies of the new contract had been distributed, but dissatisfaction with its content still remained and would continue to be an issue over which miners would strike in the future.[53]

Another large walkout occurred in the early part of 1975 over a more traditional labor-management problem. In March and April of that year approximately 14,300 employees of the North American Coal Corporation walked out of mines in Ohio, West Virginia, and Pennsylvania in a safety dispute involving the interpretation of a new helper clause in the 1974 agreement. Arbitration eventually ended the dispute but not until work stopped for approximately forty-eight hours.[54]

By far the largest and most serious walkout of 1975 took

place in the late summer of that year. The strike began on August 4 in Logan County in southern West Virginia over the suspension of a UMW local union president by the Amherst Coal Company. This suspension issue, however, was obscured as issues provoked by the strike itself became sources of contention. The strike grew as roving pickets spread throughout the county. The levying of fines against local unions and the jailing of a local union president for contempt of court by Judge K. K. Hall of the federal district court fanned the walkout throughout West Virginia and into adjoining states until at one point, 80,000 of the union's 125,000 members were off the job. By the late weeks of August the strike and its issues changed into a muddled attack on the coal companies, the federal courts, and the international union. Company policy and grievance handling, court intervention, fines, and jailings, and the international union's slowness in implementing a district grievance arbitration panel, all combined as grounds for the strike, which became a kind of catchall protest.[55] One issue, however, rose above the rest as a rallying point for the striking miners—the lack of a right-to-strike provision in the 1974 agreement.[56]

A strike of this magnitude created a difficult situation for Miller. On one hand, more than half his members were out on strike, and to disagree with them on the strike issues could mean political suicide. Yet legally, Miller had an obligation to enforce the contract and faced heavy pressure from the coal operators and the courts, backed by threats of lawsuits and fines. Again, Miller took an essentially passive role in this strike. Although he encouraged the men to go back to work and even threatened a few militants with disciplinary action by the union, his efforts had little or no effect in the settlement of the strike.[57]

The strike was a costly one for everyone concerned. The companies reported losses of 5 million tons of coal production, and the miners lost more than $26 million in wages.[58] In addition, the UMW was fined $700,000 and sued for more than $10 million as a result of the strike. To try to deal with unauthorized work stoppages in the future, Miller set up a joint UMW-BCOA committee to deal with the handling of grievances and the use of court injunctions, which in the past had been the main sources of irritation. In conjunction, the IEB adopted a "ten-point program" for dealing with wildcats that called for specific plans of action on all levels of the union.[59] The board also tried two miners for their militant role in the wildcats and subsequently suspended them from the union for one year.[60]

The international union's approach to this situation was either misdirected or simply ineffective. Again in 1976, as in the first three years of Miller's administration, the wildcat problem increased in incidence and severity. The number of man-days reported lost rose by a third to 1,950,300 as the number of walkouts increased to 2,787.[61] Although only two of these wildcats involved more than ten thousand miners, the trend was unmistakable—wildcat strikes were on the rise despite the efforts of the international union to stem the tide.[62]

The first major walkout of 1976 began on the first day of March and eventually involved 18,752 miners over a seven-day period.[63] The strike, as so many during the previous few years, began in southern West Virginia and extended into other parts of the state as well as into Virginia. The issue this time was general dissatisfaction with current black lung laws and specific opposition to a black lung bill that was pending before the U.S. House of Representatives. Miller dealt with the situation in much the same manner as he had previous walkouts, namely, by admonishing the miners from the distance of the international headquarters that such a strike would damage their cause and by bringing the leaders of the strike to the international for disciplinary hearings. The effect was uniformly the same. The miners struck anyway and only returned to work when fervor among the rank-and-file supporters diminished.[64]

The second major wildcat strike of 1976 occurred in the late summer and involved more than ninety thousand coal miners at its peak, the largest number involved in any walkout since Miller took office. Similar to the massive wildcat of the previous summer, this strike had its origin in an incident involving a local union in Kanawha County, southern West Virginia. The strike began when Local 1759 at Cabin Creek demanded that an important mine communications job be filled by a UMW member. The company refused the demand, but an arbitrator later settled the matter in the union's favor. The company, however, refused to comply with the umpire's award, citing a technicality. The union tried to have the award enforced by Judge Dennis Knapp of the federal district court, but the judge turned their appeal down saying he "hadn't the time to hear the case." The case went back to the umpire, who this time, in a vague award, ruled in favor of the company.[65]

Local 1759 struck, and within two days was slapped with a back-to-work order by the same Judge Knapp they had asked to enforce the arbitration award. The local again tried to see the judge, but once again he was too busy. When the miners refused to end the strike, Judge Knapp fined the local $50,000 for the walkout and $25,000 for each day the strike continued.[66] The strike not only continued but spread rapidly. With the use of roving pickets, mines in virtually all the eastern coal-producing states and one western state, nine states in all, walked out.[67] The strike received support from a recent Supreme Court decision that greatly weakened the coal companies' main weapon against wildcats, the injunction. In *Buffalo Forge* v. *United Steelworkers*, the Court ruled that "a federal district court cannot enjoin a local union from conducting a 'sympathy' strike to support another local." Whereas in the 1975 walkout courts hit numerous locals with injunctions and fines for striking in sympathy, in 1976, only Local 1759, locus of the strike, was subject to court injunctions.[68]

As had happened in 1975, the strike outgrew the original issue and focused its efforts on a broader issue, namely, court intervention in general and the issuance of injunctions in particular. Although the miners had recently won an important battle in this area with the Buffalo Forge decision, Judge Knapp's actions against Local 1759 were enough to ignite the volatile situation. As one Cabin Creek miner said, "When that judge gets out of the coal business, that's when we go back to work."[69]

Although the 1975 strike was termed a "right-to-strike" strike and the 1976 walkout was called an "injunction" strike, they involved very similar, if not identical, issues. Miller assumed the same role during the 1976 strike that he had assumed in previous walkouts. Although he met with groups of miners and local union officers on several occasions, his leadership did not play a crucial role in getting the miners back to work.

The strike eventually ended on August 13 after Local 1759 voted three to one to return to work.[70] The strike toll was heavy, $24 million in wages lost by the miners and $150 million in production reported lost by the coal operators.[71] The miners accomplished very little by the strike except to make clear for the second year in a row that something had to change. Most UMW members looked forward to the 1977 contract negotiations for that change.

Payroll losses to the industry's employees for the period from 1974 through 1976 totaled $242,471,100, while the industry reportedly lost 4,391,500 man-days and 47,990,000 tons in potential coal production. In addition, the union suffered a $70,729,000 loss in employer contributions to its trust fund as well as numerous fines and lawsuits.[72]

The wildcat problem was the most dramatic example of the paradox that democratic unionism brought to the UMW. The union leadership was responsible for making sure the agreement it signed on behalf of its membership was respected by that membership. It also needed to develop and enforce policies and practices within the union that benefited the interests of the entire membership. Localized, or even more widespread wildcat strikes, put the leadership in the difficult position of being legally responsible to management and morally obligated to its nonstriking members to restrain such action. Lewis could and did put down wildcats as if they were insurrections. Yet, because wildcat strikes were a popular expression by the membership, the dilemma they posed for Miller was not so easily solved.

Miller, in the course of his first term, did not take a forceful position in dealing with the wildcat situation. He did, however, provide leadership in certain areas aimed at dealing with the root problem of many wildcats, the contract and grievance procedure. During Miller's administration the UMW began a series of new, experimental education programs aimed at giving the rank and file the tools they needed to deal effectively with management in enforcing the contract and working with the grievance procedure. In addition, changes in the grievance procedure itself helped to make it a more efficient mechanism for dispute settlement. The 1974 agreement created the Arbitration Review Board, consisting of one union representative, one management representative, and one neutral member, to bring consistency and efficiency to the arbitration process. During Miller's first term both the educational program and the Arbitration Review Board met with some success, but due to both practical and political circumstances, they were received with only mixed enthusiasm.[73]

The turbulent period of strike activity occurring between 1974 and 1976 paralleled closely the chaotic leadership situation at the international level of the union caused by the constant infighting between Miller and the IEB. As this bickering consumed the leadership of the union and the constructive and progressive administration of union affairs was neglected, the poor relationship between coal management and the miners continued, and in some cases, even deteriorated. When the union continually failed to aid them in their struggle, miners in the coalfields channeled their frustrations into the independent actions of wildcat strikes.

The newfound democratic atmosphere in the UMW, brought about by the reform movement of 1972, played a major role in this period of strife. Increased democracy, without a doubt, contributed to both the political turbulence and wildcats experienced by the UMW during the reform administration. These phenomena were both troubling and dangerous to the future of the union; however, they may have been necessary evils if democracy was to continue to exist in the UMW. While certainly a negative situation in its excesses, this turbulence may have been just the fleeting adolescence of a maturing democracy.

5 The 1976 Convention

I N May 1976 the International Executive Board passed a motion to move the next United Mine Workers convention up from December 1976 to September.[1] Since the nationwide bituminous coal agreement expired in December, practical considerations justified this move. The news media billed the convention as a once-and-for-all showdown between Miller and the IEB because of the internal factionalism and the highly charged political maneuvering that occurred as the 1977 international elections approached. Miller's announcement in May 1976 that he would appeal several IEB decisions at the convention heightened this speculation.[2] The 1976 convention was a barometer of the progress democratic reform had made in the miners' union. By attempting to settle problems confronting the UMW in the forum of a democratic convention, the union was putting democracy to the test.

In his 1976 "State of the Union" address, Arnold Miller made a promise to the two thousand coal miner delegates assembled for the UMW's forty-seventh consecutive constitutional convention: "This is a democratic union and this is going to be a democratic convention. Every delegate will be given the same opportunity to speak his mind. And the decisions will be made by majority vote."[3] This pledge was met with a thunderous burst of applause. The delegates had not forgotten their struggle for democracy, and they were eager to assert themselves in the workings of their union. The 1973 convention had established democratic rights for UMW members. In 1976 the delegates were determined to exercise the democratic rights they had won.

The method by which the delegates are elected is vitally important. The delegates who met in Cincinnati were elected by the membership under the same revised representation standards that were in effect at the 1973 convention in Pittsburgh. The goals were still to represent as effectively as possible the rank and file and to allow the membership an opportunity to participate in the administration of the union through the convention. As in 1973, there were no bogus locals, nor were there staff delegates, except those who were legitimately elected by their home local. There were, however, some significant differences from the 1973 convention in the composition of the delegation that met in September 1976.

One difference was the increased number of delegates in Cincinnati and the decreased delegate-to-member ratio, which indicated a greater percentage of the union's rank and file was participating in the democratic processes of the UMW. At Pittsburgh in 1973, approximately 1,000 delegates represented an active union membership of 120,000.[4] In 1976, 1,883 delegates represented an active membership of 180,000.[5] The number of delegates increased 88 percent, while union membership increased only 50 percent. Consequently, the members-per-delegate quotient dropped from one delegate per 120 members in 1973 to one delegate per 95 members in 1976.[6] These figures, combined with the fact that 60 percent of the delegates at Cincinnati had never before attended a UMW convention, indicated that many new or previously uninvolved miners were actively participating in the affairs of the union, a step toward a more representative convention delegation.[7]

The election of delegates was one manner in which the membership at the local level became involved in the convention process. A second important area of local involvement was in the formulation and submission of resolutions for the consideration of the convention. All resolutions and reports brought to the floor by the committees theoretically derived from these local resolutions. The resolution process allowed greater membership input into the convention. This was not the case during the reign of John L. Lewis and Tony Boyle. The orchestrated nature of conventions during that period was well known by the membership. It was also well known that the submittance of any resolution not in complete accord with administration policies was a futile gesture. The small number of resolutions submitted during those years reflected this feeling of impotence on the part of the membership.[8]

The advent of democratic convention procedures in 1973, however, encouraged locals to submit any and all resolutions they believed important. The increased number of resolutions submitted by the local unions reflected the membership's desire to participate. In 1948 all the resolutions sent in amounted to 174 printed pages;[9] in 1976 resolutions submitted filled 1,431 pages.[10] The 1973 convention apparently convinced the membership that the resolutions process was an effective means of participating in the administration of their union. At Pittsburgh, the Collective Bargaining Committee received approximately 1,200 resolutions for its consideration. In Cincinnati this same committee had the monumental task of processing 5,947 resolutions.[11] This was a 400 percent rise from 1973 and indicated an increased interest in decision and policy making at the lower echelons of the union.

The changes in the convention's committee system were another of the major reforms carried over to the Cincinnati convention. In 1976 the convention utilized the committee format first used in 1973. The administration reduced the size of committees from the forty to fifty members of Lewis-Boyle years to an average of approximately twenty-five members. The Collective Bargaining Committee had the most members, thirty-eight, in order to deal with its great volume of work.[12] Only committees necessary to the work of the convention met, and there were none of the unproductive honorary committees of past UMW conventions. The international union restricted pay in accord with the precedent set in 1973.[13] Miller still retained the constitutional privilege of appointing the committee personnel. This undoubtedly was reflected in the composition of the committees. The IEB, which traditionally had seen a high percentage of their members placed on committees, had

77

only seven of its twenty-one district representatives appointed in 1976. Of these, only two were clearly and consistently members of the anti-Miller faction.[14] Politics unabashedly intervened in this important facet of convention mechanics.

By reconstructing the important elements of the convention—the delegation, the resolution process, and the committee system—the administration had laid the groundwork for a democratic convention. Beyond these new features, the mechanics of the 1976 UMW convention were similar to most union conventions. The agenda involved the presentation of committee reports, debate and discussion on these reports, and finally action, either favorable or unfavorable, on the committees' recommendations. There were, however, two exceptional factors, the convention chairman and the delegates, both of which were important influences on the character of the 1976 convention.

The chair, in many respects, determines the extent to which democracy is exercised, both on and off the convention floor. John L. Lewis, for example, ran a very tightly controlled convention. Typical of Lewis's demeanor in the chair is the following incident, which involved a challenge from the convention floor:

> Delegate Stevenson: I think everybody in this convention . . . .
> President Lewis: It does not matter what you think. The chair has ruled.[15]

Through the sheer force of his personality Lewis conveyed that it was his convention the delegates were attending. He allowed the trappings of democracy on the floor only so long as they did not interfere with his dictates.

Although in the chair, Miller was the antithesis of Lewis, his performance as chairman was just as important as Lewis's in setting the tone of the convention. Whereas Lewis was a tyrant in the chair, Miller was a mediator. If Lewis's forceful will surpressed the free expression of opinions and ideas, Miller's lack of force and willingness to let everyone have his say encouraged democracy, and at times, near-anarchy.[16]

The rules employed during the Lewis and Boyle years were

very rigid and contributed to the chair's supreme dominion over the proceedings. The Miller administration revised the convention rules to fit the democratic theme of the meetings. The new rules encouraged discussion and debate, made access to the floor easier for the delegates, and built in flexibility to allow for increased delegate involvement.[17]

The use of more democratic rules could not, by itself, ensure a democratic convention. Most delegates lacked experience in the mechanics of democracy. Early in the 1976 convention it became painfully obvious that few delegates understood the intricacies of parliamentary procedure. Miller himself lacked experience, having never attended a convention before 1973, let alone chaired one. Although assisted by a parliamentarian in Cincinnati, Miller often departed from the rules in order to allow more debate or to confirm that a vote was correct. He made frequent exceptions and allowances when delegates raised points or motions incorrectly. The parliamentary procedures that developed in the course of the convention were a uniquely adapted miner's version. Miller did not let the rules stand in the way of keeping the convention as open as possible.

Parliamentary procedure grants the chair one particularly critical responsibility, ruling on votes. The chair's judgment on votes to close debate, call for a roll call vote, or reconsider a motion, in addition to votes on issues before the convention, can influence the substance and process of a convention. Miller performed this function relatively well. For the most part, his decisions on the votes appeared fair and accurate. When Miller was uncertain on the voice vote, he would call for a standing vote. If there was any controversy on his decision, he would call for a revote immediately. As mentioned previously, the Cincinnati convention called for only one roll call vote. Roll call votes were a relatively new experience for delegates who had attended past UMW conventions. It was practically impossible to get such a vote at a Lewis or Boyle convention. The one at Pittsburgh in 1973 was the first of its kind at a UMW convention since 1936.[18]

The attitudes and actions of the delegation in Cincinnati also contributed to the character of the 1976 UMW convention. Unlike some union conventions, which serve as junkets for dutiful union officers and members, the Cincinnati convention had an air of weighty deliberation. Most delegates to the meeting approached their duties with seriousness and purposefulness. The convention considered carefully all matters brought before it. The delegates scrutinized each resolution as if they were suspicious of having something slip by. A considerable number of resolutions met with hot debate. The convention rejected numerous resolutions, and most of the committees found it necessary to report a second time.[19] This was an occurrence almost unheard of in the union until 1973.

The delegates in Cincinnati demonstrated intensity from the start. On the opening day of the convention, Secretary-Treasurer Harry Patrick tried to skip over the arduous formality of reading the convention call with a quick vote. The delegation reacted strongly to this. As if to set the precedent that nothing would be railroaded, the delegates demanded that Miller come to the chair, overrule Patrick, and compel him to read the call or conduct a roll call vote on the issue. Miller, recognizing the concern of the delegation, acceded to their wishes and had the convention call read.

> Secretary-Treasurer Patrick: The Chair rules with unanimous consent that to dispense with the reading of the Call is proper.
>
> Delegate William Youst, District 6, Local 2262: I make the motion to carry on without reading the Call as you have requested. Mr. Chairman. We don't want to hear the Call read. I think you asked the membership here if you could go ahead and by-pass it, and I think we agreed.
>
> Secretary-Treasurer Patrick: You make a motion to dispense with the reading of the Call?
>
> Mr. Youst: Yes.
>
> Secretary-Treasurer Patrick: Do I hear a second?
>
> (Chorus of "noes.")
>
> Unidentified Delegate: Second.
>
> Secretary-Treasurer Patrick: Those in favor of the motion to dispense with the reading of the Call, signify by saying "aye."

(Chorus of "ayes.")

Opposed?

(Chorus of "noes.")

The "ayes" have it.

President Miller: Let's have a little order. Let's have a little order. For what reason does the delegate rise at Mike 3?

Delegate Ed Weido, District 4, Local 6290: I ask that we have a roll call vote because of the inaccuracies of the voice vote.

(Applause.)

President Miller: Brother, would you go back to the mike? Do you want a roll call or rising vote or standing vote?

Delegate Weido: A roll call vote.

President Miller: Do you realize what a roll call vote is?

Delegate Weido: Yes, I do, Mr. Chairman. I understand that, and I think we are here to do business and not to be railroaded down the line.

(Applause.)

President Miller: Let's have some order. Let me see if we can get a consensus of where we are at here. I believe the question before this body was, did you want the Call read, and I think we ought to reaffirm, or reassess our situation here, and if you want it read, I think it would be more proper to read the Call than it would be to go through the roll call vote just to see if you are going to.

(Applause.)

If there is no objection from this delegation, I will have the Call read. If there is no objection, the Call will be read.[20]

For the most part, the delegates to the Cincinnati convention demanded a great deal of freedom within the convention process. The delegates themselves set the tone and pace of the convention. The relationship between Miller and the delegation, however, was also important in this respect. The delegates had a keen sense of when the deliberations were getting out of hand

and becoming unproductive. Miller read the delegation very well on this problem, asserting his authority to bring order only when he sensed the support of the majority. At these moments the delegates needed and welcomed a strong hand in the chair; at other times they would not tolerate such interference.

Although the 1976 convention accomplished a great deal in reforming the convention process and changing the traditional role of the delegates and the chair, it also experienced some serious problems in these same areas. One particularly serious flaw that colored the 1976 proceedings throughout was the factionalism of internal union politics.

Union politics were in the air when the meeting convened in Cincinnati. The election of international officers was scheduled for 1977 and political maneuvering had already begun for the UMW's presidential race. Miller had already announced his plans to run for reelection.[21] Vice President Trbovich had publicly acknowledged considering a run for the top office since the rift between him and Miller had become irreconcilable.[22] In addition, Lee Roy Patterson, formerly a staunch Boyle supporter and IEB member from western Kentucky, had openly solicited support since the spring of 1976. Lesser politicos jockeyed for spots on various slates, while the political opportunists sniffed the air to determine the candidate with the most potential for victory.

In his opening remarks to the delegates, John Guzek, president of host District 6, warned, "There is no room for politics in this convention."[23] The delegates did not heed his warning. Anti-Miller aspirants and their supporters were largely responsible for the turbulence that disrupted the workings of the convention in Cincinnati. There was irony in these efforts, whether planned or spontaneous, as administration foes used the democratic mechanism of freedom to dissent to show that the democratic system evolving in the union was inoperative and unproductive. These efforts culminated in an inflammatory and demagogic speech by Vice President Trbovich. In this speech Trbovich accused the administration of using political tactics that were "shades of Stalin's Russia and Hitler's Germany!"[24]

Trbovich went on to invoke one of labor's most tried and

tested tactics of division, red-baiting. He charged that the Miller administration had allowed, "the internal infiltration of the Socialistic, Revolutionary, and Communistic elements which may soon threaten to destroy [the] union."[25] This starkly political attack caused general pandemonium at one point and was responsible for an anti-Communist witch-hunt that led to the expulsion of left-wing reporters, a credentials check on delegates alleged to be Communists and therefore in violation of the UMWA constitution, and a preoccupation with exorcising the radicals from the convention delegation.[26] This greatly impeded the work of the convention. Trbovich's tirade also tainted the deliberations with the smell of politics and encouraged the political factionalism that carried over into the issues of the convention. All these factors deterred the purpose and the work of the convention and reflected negatively on Miller and his administration.

A second problem that plagued the convention was the inexperience of the delegates with the mechanics of a democratic convention. Order, in most formal democratic meetings, is achieved through the use of a parliamentary procedure. Unfamiliarity with the convention process and *Robert's Rules of Order* which governed the process, combined with the delegates' desire to participate actively, created a disorderly, slow-moving convention. One good indicator of the low productivity of the sessions is the number of irrelevant, inappropriate, or out-of-order exchanges and interruptions that occurred. For example, on the second day of the 1976 convention there were 128 such occurrences.[27] Although the pace of the meetings quickened as delegates became acclimated and informed, this number is striking when compared to past conventions. On the second day of Tony Boyle's 1968 convention no such exchanges occurred; in fact, only one delegate spoke from the floor the entire day.[28] At the 1976 Cincinnati convention approximately one hundred delegates addressed the convention on its second day, some on more than one occasion.[29] These two profoundly different types of conventions represent widely divergent points on the spectrum, one ultraefficient and undemocratic, the other very democratic and less than efficient.

A set of brief exchanges on the convention floor during the

second day of the 1976 convention illustrated the inexperience of the delegates:

President Miller: It has been moved and seconded on the adoption of the rules. The question is on the adoption of Rule 1. The fellow at Mike 5 didn't state his name.

Unidentified Delegate: Bruce Boyens, District 17, Local 6608.

President Miller: When you go to a mike, please state your name and district number. The Chair recognizes the delegate at Mike 1.

Delegate Andrew Morris, District 31, Local 5429: Mr. Chairman, did I hear you correctly say that you are now going to take up section-by-section the rules so that we can adopt them or amend them section-by-section, and not accept the entire report? Is that correct? Well, that is what I want, because I don't want the rules adopted until we have a chance to amend or agree on all of them. Thank you very much.

President Miller: The Chair recognizes the delegate at Mike 3.

Unidentified Delegate: Thank you. I appreciate this.

President Miller: State your name and local union number and district number.

Delegate Prentice Howard, Jr., District 11, Local 1015: Rule No. 4, recess and—

President Miller: Excuse me, Brother. We haven't gotten to Rule No. 4.

Delegate Howard: Okay. I'll wait then.

President Miller: We are going to take them rule-by-rule. Is there any discussion on Rule 1? The Chair recognizes the delegate at Mike 6.

Delegate Colin Simmons, District 6, Local 6271: I got a remark under 11, Rule No. 11.

President Miller: We haven't come to that yet. The Chair recognizes the delegate at Mike 7, and only those that want to address themselves to Rule 1 will be recognized.

You are out of order if you don't. The Chair recognizes the delegate at Mike 7.

Delegate Dennis Spangler, District 29, Local 7086: I would like to stay here by the mike. I've got something on Rule No. 4 and something else, but could we carry on in a faster pace and get this out of the way? We are still on No. 1.

President Miller: If you are on No. 1, address yourself to No. 1, and we will be moving. The Chair recognizes the delegate at Mike 8.

Delegate Joseph Tate, District 28, Local 2166: I have a question on Rule 13, if I might be in order.

President Miller: You are out of order. Anyone that gets to a mike and addresses themselves to any other rule except Rule 1 is going to be ruled out of order. The Chair will recognize someone at the mikes to address themselves to Rule 1.[30]

Notwithstanding this atmosphere that *Business Week* compared to "Portugal after it was released from dictatorship,"[31] the 1976 convention produced some substantive improvements in the area of union law and policy that aided the push for a more democratic union. Foremost among these were constitutional amendments that wrote into the union bylaws reforms giving more control than ever to the rank and file. A strong sentiment existed among the delegates that to ensure membership control over the administration a number of changes must be made. Many delegates held the opinion that a decentralization of responsibilities and of the power that goes with responsibility must occur. Many delegates were also of the opinion that the membership's ultimate weapon, the vote, must cover more, if not all of the office and staff positions at every level of the union's administration. These ideas were at the roots of many resolutions considered.

The convention took action to decentralize the duties of the union government in two major areas, the dues system and the organizing and safety departments. At the time of the convention the international union collected the members' dues and distributed them according to union law. Since taking office, the new administration had redesigned and computerized the accounting system at international headquarters. The new system had proved inefficient and costly. In a motion that signaled a lack of confidence in the international's ability to correct the situation, the convention approved a measure in which it "resolved that the collection of dues shall revert to the secretary-treasurer of each district."[32] This measure removed the district's dependence on the international for its funds and made the international dependent on the districts for its monies. This, combined with district autonomy, undoubtedly gave the districts a degree of independence never before realized in the history of the union.

The most heated debate of the convention occurred over the issue of who should control the union's organizing and safety programs. The administration argued that decentralized organizing and safety programs would greatly weaken the union's organizing strategy and its drive for safety improvements. In a very close and controversial vote the delegation approved a measure to leave organizing and safety under the aegis of the international.[33] Although the vote buried the topic temporarily, it left the convention bitterly divided.

One of the constitutional reforms that held great potential for increased membership control over the policies of the union involved the practice that was nearly as old as the union of presidential appointments to convention committees. This presidential privilege was a powerful weapon for gaining control over the union's convention. The convention abolished this practice when it rejected a Constitution Committee recommendation and adopted an amendment that provided for the election of committee members at district conventions where every local would have representation.[34]

Another area of reform that sought to bring the international level of the union under the scrutiny of the membership focused on the International Executive Board. The IEB was alleged by Miller to have been uncooperative and unproductive in recent years, and the Constitution Committee reported resolutions that would make it possible for the membership to observe the activities of the IEB. The resolutions passed by the convention called for all IEB meetings in the future to be open to UMW members and for meetings to be held at various locations in the coalfields where union members would have easy access to them. In addition, the minutes of all IEB meetings would be mailed to each local union and would be available for all union members to read.[35] This opened to membership scrutiny a body that had in the past operated behind closed doors.

The convention passed a few other constitutional reforms of lesser importance but also calculated to open up the union to the membership. These included reforms of the contract ratification process and the opening up of district executive boards in the same manner and with the same rationale as for the IEB meetings.[36]

Central to the UMW's newly defined collective bargaining system was the role of the convention in formulating the initial demands and priorities that the negotiating team takes to the bargaining table. This function of the convention is probably second in importance only to the function of constitutional revision. The increased interest in this function was demonstrated by the 400 percent rise in resolutions dealing with collective bargaining between 1973 and 1976. Although the convention bargaining guidelines are not binding, the international officers who negotiate the contract cannot ignore the guidelines because of the likelihood that the convention and membership demands will probably closely coincide. With a membership ratification looming at the end of negotiations, the convention guidelines are an important mandate.

With the industrywide bituminous coal agreement scheduled to expire in December 1977, contract demands were an important topic in Cincinnati. The political overtones of the debates on other issues did not infuse the discussions on bargaining, and the convention showed unity on these issues. Although the "dream sheet" that evolved was long, the administration was made aware of what the top priorities should probably be in 1977.[37]

One of the most significant contract goals endorsed by the convention was the right to strike over certain local contractual issues. The delegates passed a resolution that, if included in the contract, would give members at the local level the right to choose to arbitrate a local grievance or to strike over the issue. This was a unique approach to dispute settlement and one that the coal operators opposed vehemently. The convention also passed resolutions directing the union's negotiators to seek a six-hour day, a "substantial" wage increase, additional personal leave and holidays, a system of graduated vacation, a seniority system based on length of service alone, and additional paid time off for union safety and contract enforcement training.[38]

The remaining issues brought before the convention did not involve, in themselves, the democratization of the union or the union convention. These issues included health and safety, organizing, pensions, and political matters. The delegation, however, did not take lightly any of these reports. There was substantial debate on issues in all of these areas and, in many cases, the delegates rejected the resolutions and sent them back to committee. Democracy at the 1976 convention applied to all issues in all areas, and the delegates accepted, if not relished, their democratic responsibilities. The decisions made by the delegation should, in practice, become the policies of the international union. The international administration had to attempt to carry out the mandates of the convention or face an electorate infused with a new sense of power over the governance of their union.

The convention mechanism played an active and important role in the Miller administration's efforts at reform during his first term in office. It was responsible for progress in two important areas. First, reforms at the 1973 and 1976 conventions have completely transformed the convention process itself. Second, the Miller administration made substantive reforms in the union's structure, administration, and policies.

Probably the most important reforms concerning convention procedure itself were those affecting the convention committee. The elimination of nonfunctional committees and committee seats and the election of committee members were significant changes. In addition, a new set of rules and new approaches to the roles of the chairperson and the delegates transformed the form and function of the convention. These fundamental changes were accompanied by a number of problems, including the inexperience of the delegates and leadership in the democratic process and the increase in factionalism that divided the union.

The substantive reforms in the union's structure, administration, and policies achieved through the conventions during Miller's first term touched all areas of the union. Foremost among these changes was the restoration of district autonomy, including the right of districts to elect their own officials. In addition, the conventions overhauled the entire internal election process, opened the deliberations of the IEB to the scrutiny of the membership, and completely revamped the union's collective bargaining process. The delegates also reshaped the UMW's policies concerning political action and health and safety.

The experience of the UMW during Miller's initial term demonstrated the effectiveness of the union convention as a means of encouraging greater participation in the administration of the union by the rank and file. Between 1972 and 1977, the miners' union was transformed, not by the edict of a select hierarchy, but by the membership through the democratic convention process.

6 Toward a Second Term

ALTHOUGH generally a successful democratic exercise, the 1976 UMW convention was pervaded by union politics. Billed as a political showdown for control of the international union, the convention only polarized the factions further while muddling the issues. The convention did, however, set a date for the upcoming 1977 international elections at which time the conflict could be fought openly and perhaps settled once and for all. Although campaigning for the June 14, 1977, election was not scheduled to begin formally before January, the campaign period actually began immediately after the convention. This situation brought chaos to the international as politicos jockeyed for positions and candidates began to build campaign machines.

On September 30, 1976, at about the halfway point of the UMW convention in Cincinnati, Secretary-Treasurer Harry Patrick held a press conference in the twentieth floor Presidential Suite of the Netherlands-Hilton Hotel. Asked about the incongruity of the secretary-treasurer occupying the Presidential Suite, Patrick said he was there only because "Arnold had looked at it and turned it down in favor of the Imperial Suite."[1] Arnold Miller had come a long way since the rank-and-file days of 1972. Despite the hardship of his first term, he had grown comfortable with his position of authority and the accouterments of power. Miller had pledged in 1972 that he would serve only one term.[2] In March 1975, however, Miller officially announced his plans for a reelection bid, declaring, "Some of the programs that I've started now will require me to run one more term."[3] After the convention, critics charged that Miller's plans for reelection became the chief item of business at international headquarters as Miller formulated political strategies and tested loyalties for the upcoming campaign and election.[4]

In the weeks after the convention Miller revealed an almost paranoid suspicion of the loyalties of many of his closest aides and allies. Patrick, heretofore Miller's highest ranking and most loyal aide and ally, ranked foremost on his list of possible Brutuses. According to a senior staffer, many Miller decisions during this period had at their root the belief that Patrick was clandestinely plotting a campaign for the presidency. Miller also apparently believed his staff was secretly aiding Patrick in this conspiracy.

The first bombshell, in what was to become just another front in the UMW's ongoing internecine war, exploded the week following the convention when Miller abruptly fired two of his top aides, Ed Burke, executive assistant to the president, and Bernie Aronson, director of publications and press relations. Critics said Miller feared that neither Burke nor Aronson would aid his reelection bid and would instead support Patrick.[5] According to Burke, Miller stated that he dismissed the two men for "betraying the trust of the union president— being disloyal and failing to carry out directives."[6] Although no specific charges were ever made against the two employees, Miller, in a press release issued after the firings, termed speculation that his dismissals of Burke and Aronson were politically motivated "absurd and totally without foundation in fact." He went on to say that the dismissal was "based on my assessment of their job performance. It was not based on who they support for union office."[7] One union insider stated that Miller judged Aronson to be incompetent, a charge opened to speculation when the vice president of the United States, Walter Mondale, hired Aronson as his chief speechwriter.

Although not directly involved in the firings, Patrick became involved in the controversy as a result of an incident on October 8. The incident involved a written directive issued by Miller stating that no one could remove packages from international headquarters without the contents being subjected to a search. Miller apparently wished to prevent the removal of union documents from the building. On October 8, Aronson attempted to remove several boxes of personal belongings. Patrick allegedly searched the boxes personally and subsequently refused to allow one of Miller's aides to inspect them. "All it came down to," according to Patrick, "was if I was going to allow an appointed staff man to question my worth as an International officer since President Miller was not in the building."[8] Miller viewed Patrick's actions as insubordination. He authorized a special commission composed of two IEB members, Frank Clements and J. B. Trout, to investigate the incident and determine if Patrick had disobeyed the order, thus "interfering with the constitutional powers of the president."[9] A member of the UMW staff reported that in late November, after a short presentation by Clements and Trout, the IEB absolved Patrick of any wrongdoing in the incident.

From the time of the MFD convention in 1972 through the roughest times of the first administration, Patrick had been a staunch Miller ally. The events of October and November 1976, however, had a tremendous effect on the relationship between Miller and Patrick. They marked the first serious public rift between the two officers, which appeared to be the turning point in their relationship.

A siege atmosphere fell over the headquarters. Miller became increasingly suspicious of the activities of his staff and officers. He changed the locks on the headquarters building to keep fired employees out. He centralized control of all union functions in his office, ironically a tactic used by the autocratic John L. Lewis in the consolidation of his kingdom. Miller forbid staff to work in the building during weekends without permission and ordered the toll-free long-distance telephone lines turned off during those times in order to have a record of calls made. In addition, all staff travel plans had to pass across his desk for approval. In order to enforce his directives Miller hired three additional $20,000-a-year security men, labeled "international representatives," to prowl the UMW building. In addition to these sudden changes, Miller personally began to handle all press queries during this period.[10]

Former aides and supporters viewed Miller's behavior as irrational; some regarded the president as "incredibly paranoid," and said that he was "seeking an enemy under every bed." His critics pointed to an incident in early December in which Miller reportedly had the door to the office of his personal secretary removed from the hinges. Hearing reports of closed-door conversations between her and Patrick, Miller suspected his secretary of secretly plotting against him and had the door removed to end such conversations. In addition, Miller allegedly ordered the heat in Patrick's office turned off in order to make him uncomfortable.[11] When asked about his former ally's state of mind during this period Patrick said, "I'm not a doctor so I can't say if he's sick or not. What I can say is unfortunately he reminds me of Hitler in his last days when he gathered all his lieutenants together in the bunker."[12]

The tense and restrictive atmosphere at international headquarters brought the work of the union almost to a standstill. Important job vacancies went unfilled, and the morale of staff and office workers plummeted. Infighting continued and even erupted into violence when a Miller aide assaulted an allegedly disloyal UMW lawyer in his office.[13] Perhaps the greatest loss of this period was that of many of the bright, young reformers, both miners and nonminers, who had played a large part in turning the union around. The insecure and unproductive atmosphere of the UMW during this period, brought on in part by Miller's actions, was undoubtedly responsible for the many resignations that ensued in late 1976 and early 1977.

In the months following the firings of Burke and Aronson, Tom Bethell, UMW research director and a key figure in the 1974 contract talks, and Rick Bank, UMW attorney, executive assistant to Miller, and also a key figure in the 1974 negotiations, resigned. These departures left virtually none of the support staff who had helped negotiate the 1974 agreement. With the resignations of economist Tom Woodruff and the remaining research staff, the important UMW research department ceased to function. The resignations of several staff attorneys, including Bank, Davitt McAteer, Ellen Chapnick, and Rich Trumka, seriously depleted the essential UMW legal department. The organizing department lost its director, Tom Pysell, as well as a top administrative aide, while the press department lost its one remaining member, Phil Sparks. One staff member estimated that, all told, more than a third of the sixty-member staff either jumped or were pushed off the Miller ship during 1976 and early 1977.[14]

Given the atmosphere at UMW headquarters during this period, Miller was unable to fill the many job vacancies, let alone attract the kind of bright and dynamic individuals who once had manned the international union. If work at the headquarters had been slowed by infighting before the 1976 convention, it came to a grinding halt for the nine months from the September convention to the June election.

The staff firings and resignations, the Patrick insubordination trial, and the generally poor state of the union during the period after the convention terminated the already deteriorating relationship between Arnold Miller and Harry Patrick. Patrick had publicly maintained his allegiance throughout the 1976 convention, even though rumor that a break was occurring had already begun to leak out. By December 1976, the break was public, and in early January of 1977 Patrick officially announced his plans to oppose Miller in the upcoming international elections.[15] Thus Miller's suspicions about Patrick were realized. Whether Patrick's turnabout was a self-fulfilling prophesy for Miller, brought about by the president's actions and behavior after the convention, or whether Patrick had harbored secret ambitions to unseat Miller remains problematic. In either case, the insubordination charges, coupled with the other incidents, provided Patrick a plausible excuse to break with Miller.

Although the break between Miller and Patrick did not occur until late 1976, battle lines for the 1977 election began to take shape at least as early as 1975 when Miller announced his plans to seek reelection to another five-year term.[16] At the same time, Lee Roy Patterson, Miller's chief nemesis, was emerging as the man most likely to carry the banner of the anti-Miller faction into the forthcoming elections. When Vice President Mike Trbovich decided against running, apparently due to his rejection at the 1976 convention, Patterson's campaign became all but official. Although Patterson did not formally announce his candidacy until October 1976, the "Patterson for President" campaign materials that circulated openly at the 1976 convention indicated he probably had made his decision before that time.[17] Patrick either labored long over his decision or delayed his announcement, not making his election bid public until January 14, 1977.[18]

On December 21, 1976, at the Heart O' Town Motel in Charleston, West Virginia, Arnold Miller announced his slate of candidates. Much had changed since his last such announcement at the 1972 MFD convention in Wheeling. His slate for 1977 combined old and new. After "half a dozen Board members and district presidents" allegedly wished him well but refused to run with him, Miller recruited two little known miner-staffers for the number two and three spots on his ticket.[19] Miller picked his closest administrative aide, Sam Church, as the vice presidential candidate and chose Bill Esselstyn, an employee of the UMW political branch, as his candidate for secretary-treasurer.[20]

Miller's running mates added little to his campaign except a touch of irony. Although an ally turned enemy in the vice president's job had plagued Miller throughout his first term, Miller chose an enemy turned ally as his vice presidential candidate for the 1977 election race. In 1972, Sam Church had been a Boyle enthusiast and vigorously opposed Miller. After Boyle's loss, Church repented and became a staunch Miller supporter, rising to the international staff in 1976. A hulking man with a hot temper, the forty-year-old Church, originally from southwestern Virginia, proved his loyalty to Miller in December 1976 by assaulting UMW lawyer Rick Bank for allegedly leaking unfavorable information about Miller to the press. Lacking significant demonstrated administrative skill or political expertise, Church's newfound devotion and availability constituted his primary credentials for the vice presidency.[21]

Miller's pick for the secretary-treasurer spot also had an ironic touch. His first administration had been criticized constantly for its inability to handle financial affairs efficiently. The inexperience of Harry Patrick contributed to this problem. Yet in 1977, Miller picked a candidate who had little previous experience or training in financial affairs. Bill Esselstyn, a thirty-year-old miner from western Pennsylvania, had spent only six years in the mines before joining the union's staff. Although enthusiastic and confident, Esselstyn lacked significant previous experience in either contract negotiations or financial management.[22] Since both came from already strong pro-Miller districts, neither Church nor Esselstyn added political strength to Miller's slate.

Patterson's slate of candidates, announced in October 1976, reflected politically more logical choices. Running with Patterson for vice president was Gene Mitchell, the elected IEB member from District 12 in Illinois, a district that voted almost two to one for Miller in 1972. In addition to being a favorite son in a strong Miller region, Mitchell had maintained a low profile while opposing Miller in the IEB wars and was a stable, experienced union officer. Patterson picked Carroll Rogers, a district executive board (not to be confused with the International Executive Board) member in District 31, northern West Virginia, as his candidate for secretary-treasurer. Rogers was a solid choice. Well thought of by miners of all political persuasions, Rogers hailed from Harry Patrick's home district, a Miller stronghold in 1972.[23] Here again, it appeared Patterson hoped his candidate would balance the opposition's strength in the running mate's home district, while at the same time, being acceptable to miners in other districts.

Harry Patrick's reluctance to oppose Miller, for fear that they would split the vote and allow Patterson to win, provided the other two candidates with a head start in the campaign. In spite of this handicap, Patrick still put together a slate of highly capable individuals. His vice presidential running mate was Mike Tamtom, president of District 18 in western Canada. A bright and articulate miner, Tamtom, at thirty-eight, had experience as an administrator and negotiator. Since District 18 was not covered by the BCOA agreement, Tamtom had responsibility for negotiating separate contracts for the miners in his district. In this capacity he had earned a reputation as a tough, skillful bargainer.[24] Don Yurgec of District 12 in Illinois, was Patrick's candidate for secretary-treasurer. Yurgec, also thirty-eight, had held numerous local union positions and had worked previously with Patrick at international headquarters, dealing directly with the dues system and other union financial matters.[25]

Although well qualified, Patrick's slate lacked political appeal. Tamtom and Yurgec were virtual unknowns among miners. Tamtom hailed from one of the smallest, most isolated districts in the union, while Yurgec came from a district in which Patrick already had strong support. Despite his five-year tenure as an international officer, Patrick was not so well known as either Miller or Patterson. Tamtom and Yurgec could not help Patrick overcome this handicap. Rumors surfaced during the campaign that Patrick had wanted to put together a slate with Nick DeVince, IEB member from District 5 in western Pennsylvania, and Ken Dawes, district president in Illinois, both more visible figures within the UMW. If this ticket had materialized it would have probably made for a stronger slate.

The 1977 international elections began with a nominations process conducted at the local level. Local union meetings, set aside for this purpose, took place during a nomination period designated by the UMWA constitution. A candidate was nominated for international union office by obtaining the required number of local union endorsements. Each local union voted, and the candidate receiving the greatest number of votes for that office received the local's nomination. Candidates for president, vice president, and secretary-treasurer needed the endorsement of at least twenty-five local unions to appear on the ballot, while candidates for auditor and teller required at least ten local nominations. When the 1976 convention rescheduled the elections for June 14, 1977, it set the nominating period for January 15 to March 1, 1977.[26]

When the union's tellers tabulated the nominations in March, official results showed that more local unions had nominated Patterson than Miller and Patrick combined. During the month and a half of the nominations process, Patterson collected 362 local endorsements, compared to 245 for Miller and 107 for Patrick.[27] While all three had easily gathered enough nominations to appear on the ballot, Patterson claimed the results had great significance in that they indicated the rank and file desired a change in leadership.[28] Although the results indeed proved that Patterson was a strong candidate, they were not the accurate barometers of rank-and-file sentiment he claimed. The quorum for all local nominating meetings was seven, unless provided for otherwise in the local's bylaws.[29] Thus, because most locals have membership in the hundreds and some in the thousands, there was the possibility of a small turnout misrepresenting the sentiments of the majority. As traditionally was the case with local union meetings, the turnout at many of the nomination sessions was small. In one local of more than five hundred members, Patterson won the nomination by receiving just eighteen votes, while in another local with eighteen hundred members, Patterson won with forty-three votes. Overall, Patrick estimated that only 2 to 5 percent of the rank and file participated in the nominations. One need only look at the results of the 1972 election in which Boyle received 68 percent of the nominations and only 44 percent of the vote to see that nomination results have not necessarily predicted rank-and-file opinion.[30]

Nominated at the same time as the candidates for the three top international offices were candidates for eleven lesser international posts, including vice president for pensioner affairs, three eastern auditors, three eastern tellers, one auditor and one teller from the west, and one auditor and one teller from Canada. Although the candidates formed slates before the nominations, the union did not officially recognize the slates until after the nomination period. The 1976 UMWA constitution stated, "In order to form a slate, there shall be mutual agreement to do so among all fourteen candidates."[31] The main advantage of running with a full slate was that a voter could vote a straight ticket by making one check on the ballot rather than making several marks for a split ticket. But in order to gain this advantage a ticket needed a duly nominated candidate for each of the fourteen positions. This constitutional provision became a source of great controversy in the course of the election.

After the nominations period the international tellers, whose task it was to run the election, declared that only two groups of candidates qualified as official slates, one headed by Harry Patrick and one by Arnold Miller. They ruled that the third group, headed by Lee Roy Patterson, failed to qualify because it lacked the fourteen candidates required by the constitution. Although Patterson did at one point have a full slate of fourteen candidates, the withdrawal of his Canadian auditor and teller left him with only twelve, not enough to qualify for slate privileges. This decision had ramifications in at least two areas. Most important, only the Patrick and Miller tickets would be listed on the ballots as slates; whereas, the Patterson candidates were listed in a third column headed nonslate candidates. In order to vote for either the Patrick or Miller ticket, it was necessary to make a mark only in the straight ticket block provided; however, in order to vote for the Patterson candidates it was necessary to place a mark beside each candidate's name. In addition, the tellers ruled that the Patterson candidates could not pool space provided for them in the *UMW Journal*, a privilege accorded the Patrick and Miller teams. This controversy was not particularly crucial since all the Patterson candidates were lumped together in the nonslate section of the *Journal*, which accomplished the same purpose.[32]

The slate question gave rise to two additional controversies. The first involved the qualifications to run for union office of one of the candidates on Miller's slate and, thus, the legitimacy of Miller's slate status. In May, Patterson charged that Tony Testa, a security guard at UMW headquarters running for teller on Miller's slate, was ineligible because he had not paid the proper union dues. If Testa was disqualified, Miller's ticket would lose its status on the ballot as a slate. Even though the IEB voted to disqualify Testa, the international tellers, with final authority on election matters, ruled him eligible as a candidate. Patterson took his complaint to court where a Washington judge dismissed the action as "nit-picking." After the teller's action on the Testa matter, Patterson charged all three tellers with conflict of interest since they were simultaneously administering the election while running as candidates, two of them on the Patrick slate and one with Miller. Patterson called for a union trial of the three.[33] Since no constitutional provision banned this dual role, the trial never materialized. These, and other issues, arose later as Patterson's grounds for demanding an election rerun.

Throughout the preelection period, the candidates' campaigns were less visible than the controversies surrounding the election's mechanics. Whereas the 1972 contest between MFD candidate Miller and Boyle captured the imagination and interest of miners and nonminers alike, the 1977 election met with apathy as disillusioned reformers and disgusted miners grew weary of the internal backbiting. With enthusiasm and manpower split three ways and outsiders almost absent, the 1977 election battle proved only a shadow of the struggle that occurred in 1972.

Miller conducted his campaign in the same manner as he had led the union, with a low-key, detached, almost half-hearted approach. Only the infighting between himself and his campaign staff made headlines. His 1977 campaign consisted largely of orchestrated appearances at gatherings guaranteeing substantial audiences, a definite change from the style he employed during his first election bid. In 1972, Miller traveled the coalfields, going from mine to mine in an effort to meet the membership personally. By visiting the mine bathhouses where miners congregated to prepare for work or to clean up at the shift change, Miller was able to get his message across to UMW members directly.[34] There was less bathhouse-to-bathhouse, shift-change mingling in 1977, and the pace of Miller's campaign was comparatively easy. In addition, Miller refused to appear at any of the four televised debates with the other candidates. Consequently, few UMW members got a first-hand glimpse of Miller during the campaign. The campaign itself was something of a paradox for a candidate "totally committed to winning the election and serving a second term as president of the UMW."[35] Miller's approach to the race, as well as his leadership performance in his first five years as president, can be better understood by examining his personality. Thomas N. Bethell, former UMW research director and aide to Miller during the 1972 campaign and throughout most of his first administration, described Arnold Miller:

> He was never a man who enjoyed slugging it out toe-to-toe in the brawling give-and-take of union politics. Miller was a quiet man, intelligent, concerned, ambitious but not aggressive about his ambitions.[36]

Yet to conclude that Miller's seemingly unaggressive campaign simply reflected his personality would be to underestimate Miller the politician. Liberal activist, Joseph Rauh, who worked with Miller in 1972 said, "Arnold Miller may look like a naïve guy, but he's as shrewd a politician as I have ever seen."[37] Having battled the incumbent Boyle five years earlier, Miller undoubtedly had a fair appreciation of the power of the incumbency. In union politics the advantage of the incumbency is particularly great due to the apathy of many union voters and the lack of exposure of most candidates for union office. Harry Patrick judged the incumbency to be worth 30 percent of the vote.[38] Realizing the strength of an incumbent going into an election, Miller probably decided that exposure beyond a limited point would not aid, and could potentially harm, him.

If Miller, himself, did not make these political observations, his hired campaign staff probably did. Whereas dedicated rank-and-file miners and volunteer activists and idealists staffed Miller's 1972 campaign, his 1977 campaign was largely engineered by the high-powered Washington public relations firm of Rothstein and Buckley.[39] Consultants from this public relations firm reportedly made the decision not to participate in the debates. In addition, Miller's printed campaign material, including that which appeared in the *UMW Journal*, had the slick, professional touch of a Madison Avenue advertising agency and was undoubtedly produced by his public relations people.

While Miller claimed the mantle of rank-and-file candidate, it was obvious that his rank-and-file image was professionally devised. Athough the campaign involved rank-and-file miners at the grass roots level, hired publicists called the shots. It was difficult to determine exactly where Miller's financial support came from. Miller claimed it came largely from the membership of the union and published lists of donations to prove it.[40] Yet Miller fund raisers in Washington catered largely to well-known and often well-heeled liberals outside the labor movement.[41]

As befitted a challenger, Lee Roy Patterson ran a more active campaign, concentrating his efforts on attacking the present administration. In so doing, he dealt with both his competitors in one fell swoop. Essentially Patterson's campaign extended the critical outlook he had displayed on the IEB during the last three years. By continually criticizing and opposing both Miller and Patrick, Patterson had made a name for himself. Apparently he hoped the same tactics would win him the presidency of the union. Patterson combined headline-grabbing charges ("Patterson Says Elections Ballots Are Rigged"),[42] suits, and threats, with bathhouse campaigning and televised debates to air his vitriolic attacks on Miller and Patrick.[43]

As expected, Patterson won the support of the men who had joined him previously in attacking the Miller administration. Gene Mitchell was a running mate, while Andrew Morris, a vitriolic Miller foe, acted as treasurer and fund raiser for the campaign. Mike Trbovich, retiring UMW vice president and former Miller ally, actively campaigned for the challenger. At various times, Patterson claimed the support of fifteen or sixteen of the twenty-one IEB members. Many of these officers, as well as lesser district officials in many areas, endorsed and worked for Patterson's election. Chuck Baker, the publicity specialist behind I. W. Abel's 1965 election victory in the United Steelworkers (USW), headed Patterson's campaign. Baker's link with the USW, itself, became an election issue late in the campaign.[44]

Patterson's campaign also involved the USW on another front. Toward the end of the campaign, the *Wall Street Journal* reported that Patterson had accepted a four to five thousand dollar campaign contribution from top USW officials, including retiring president I. W. Abel.[45] This information, combined with a Patterson blunder at a Washington news conference, in which he stated that "if elected, he would be willing to consider affiliation with the Steelworkers," opened the way for charges that Patterson planned to merge the union with the USW.[46] The Patrick camp harped on this issue continually in the last few days of the campaign. One piece of Patrick campaign literature ran the heading "Should Our Union Be Taken over by the Steelworkers? Lee Roy Patterson Says YES. Harry Patrick Says NO!"[47]

Harry Patrick's campaign effort suffered from its late start as well as from the unknown candidates on its slate. Whereas each of the other candidates had a built-in constituency from the start, Miller the incumbent vote and Patterson the anti-Miller vote, Patrick started virtually from scratch with only a handful of supporters. In many ways, Patrick's campaign had much in common with the 1972 MFD crusade, taking more of a positive, grass roots approach than the campaigns of the other two candidates. Patrick did not have the means to hire a professional public relations outfit, and he was, by virtue of his association with the Miller administration, in no position to take the easy negative approach used by Patterson. Patrick believed he had to come face to face with as many miners as possible. He believed that in a one-on-one situation he could convince doubters that he could do the job.[48] Patrick set about doing this by conducting an exhaustive tour of bathhouses, traveling from mine to mine, and resting between shift changes. He also took every opportunity to debate publicly, usually with Patterson. In conjunction with this grass roots approach Patrick "launched an ambitious direct-mail effort that put more than 100,000 pieces of material into the hands of the voters."[49]

Patrick staffed his campaign to a large degree with UMW members who, at one time, had been a part of the Miller administration. These miners were bitterly disappointed by Miller's performance and saw Patrick as the only hope for the continued advance of the union. Patrick's organization also included some nonminer ex-staff members who had either been purged or had resigned their posts in the administration. Tom Bethell, Tom Woodruff, and Martha Spence of the research department and Rick Bank and Ed Burke, former executive assistants to Miller, were among this group.[50] Many young miners backed Patrick, a significant factor considering the declining average age of the UMW membership.[51] Patrick received little meaningful support from the middle-level district officers of the union hierarchy. Many of these opposed Miller and supported Patterson; those who opposed Patterson supported Miller, often simply because they felt it was a bad political risk to support Patrick.[52]

Patrick's campaign suffered from a lack of funds. Liberal activists hesitated to support Patrick for fear he would split the vote with Miller and open the door for a Patterson victory. Joe

Rauh, who had been active in the MFD movement, did not throw his considerable weight behind Patrick until a poll, commissioned by Patrick's staff late in the campaign,showed that Patrick would take more votes away from Patterson than Miller.[53] Although his endorsement may have led to a late influx of contributions, liberal outsiders did not become involved to the degree they were in 1972. At the campaign's end Patrick had reportedly acquired nearly $30,000 in debts in his run for the presidency.[54]

One aspect of the 1977 campaign, unprecedented in the UMW, involved a number of debates broadcast across the coalfields by radio and television. Perhaps inspired by the 1976 Ford-Carter confrontations, these debates provided an opportunity for the presidential candidates to reach a far greater number of voters than ordinarily possible with the traditional bathhouse campaign approach. This gave coal miners their first chance to see the candidates, if not in person, at least on video tape. The four debates broadcast had great potential for informing the rank and file, but this potential was not realized because of President Miller's failure to appear at even one of the debates. Patrick and Patterson attended three of the debates, one at Point Pleasant, West Virginia, on April 2, a second at Beckley, West Virginia, on May 22, and a third held in the Huntington-Charleston, West Virginia, area on June 5. Miller sent a stand-in, secretary-treasurer candidate Bill Esselstyn, for a fourth debate held May 19 in Norton, Virginia, which both Patrick and Patterson attended. The somewhat transparent reasons Miller gave for ducking the debates included conflicts with union business and campaign schedules, but political considerations undoubtedly kept him from attending. Miller publicly stated he felt confident as the incumbent and in all probability reasoned that he had little if anything to gain from such encounters. Patrick generally gained from these debates, while Patterson lost, especially at the June 5 debate where Patrick harped on Patterson's acceptance of the USW contributions and his openness to a UMW-USW merger.[55]

The 1977 election campaign was above all a campaign of personalities. If there was one pivotal issue, it was the leadership ability of each candidate. Only vague and general platforms existed. Miller ran on the accomplishments of his administration; Patterson ran on the failures of Miller's administration; and Patrick ran on the future. Distractions became an important strategy of the challengers. Patterson sued and accused both of the other candidates, and Patrick exploited the possibility of Patterson giving away the union, while attempting to convince everyone of the fragility of Miller's sanity and judgment.[56]

Throughout the campaign Miller maintained a dignity and aloofness that only an incumbent could afford. He shrewdly dwelled on the substantial accomplishments of his administration, the return of democracy to the union and the 1974 contract. Although he achieved these gains early in his administration with considerable assistance from now-departed aides, Miller took full credit for them, while shifting the blame for any failures on others.

The only substantial issues raised during the campaign centered on three areas, the problem of wildcat strikes and contract enforcement, the financial state of the union and its Welfare and Retirement Funds, and the upcoming 1977 negotiations. In the first area, Miller supported, as did the other two candidates, the inclusion of a limited right-to-strike provision in the next contract. Although Miller had not been a real advocate of this concept before the campaign, it would have been politically dangerous to take any other stance. A right-to-strike provision would allow a local to vote on a grievance to decide whether to submit it to the grievance procedure or whether to conduct a local strike over the issue. The vote would prevent a few individuals from picketing a mine since a majority would have to approve the strike. The proposed provision undoubtedly had many rough edges, but the stance remained popular among the membership.[57]

On the second issue, Miller publicly recognized that some difficulties with the union's and the Funds' finances existed, but blamed them on Patrick's financial mismanagement and the wildcat problem. He stated, moreover, that the problems were not particularly severe and that they did not endanger the union in any way. In approaching the third issue, the upcoming contract negotiations, Miller simply relied on "his" perfor-

105

mance at the bargaining table in 1974. Miller pointed to improvements in the contract, compared it to the 1971 agreement, and argued that if he did it once he could do it again.[58]

Patterson's campaign was essentially negative on the issues as well as on personalities. When he did get down to substantive considerations he could not escape framing them critically. Patterson supported the right-to-strike provision, calling it a necessity because of the lack of leadership in contract enforcement by the Miller administration. He further castigated Miller for not winning this provision in 1974. The political buckshot Patterson most often used in his assaults upon Miller and Patrick, however, involved the financial state of the union. Quoting complicated financial figures in a simplistic manner, Patterson attempted to make the case that Miller and Patrick had taken the union from financial strength to near-bankruptcy. He also made an issue of the proposed sale of UMW property in Washington, D.C., for what he claimed was less than par value, all with the intent of proving financial mismanagement on the part of the Miller administration. Although Patterson based most of his accusations on emotional or sensational appeals, one of his financial allegations, that a cutback in the level of health benefits was forthcoming, did materialize shortly after the election.[59]

Patterson's strategy in the area of contract negotiations involved a concerted attack on the agreement negotiated by the Miller administration in 1974. Problems had arisen with the 1974 agreement. The grievance procedure did not function, and the agreement lacked a right-to-strike provision. The pension system did not treat all retired miners equally, and the Funds had become financially insecure. Many miners found the contract's language difficult to understand and work with. Patterson preyed on these dysfunctions, while ignoring the substantial achievements of the agreement. He also made flashy, unrealistic contract promises. Most eye-catching among these was the hundred-dollar-a-day pledge, which meant that Patterson would have to convince the coal operators to grant an increase of approximately 66 percent over the 1974 average. Patterson also promised, in vague terms, hazard pay underground, more time off with pay, and a royalty increase to strengthen the Welfare and Retirement Funds. These were only three of a laundry list of twenty-eight promises made by Patterson.[60]

While Patterson employed accusatory methods in his campaign, he in turn received from both other candidates the same kind of mud he was so adept at slinging. Patrick remained throughout Patterson's most vocal accuser, constantly reminding miners of Patterson's close association with Boyle and of his opposition to many of the democratic innovations introduced since 1972. Patrick also skillfully exploited Patterson's Steelworker association, the USW donations he received, and his statement about being open to a USW-UMW merger. Miller dwelled less on the negative, but did portray Patterson as a remnant of the regressive old guard that had stood in the way of progress for the last four years.[61]

Harry Patrick's campaign had a far greater focus on issues than that of either of the other candidates. He could not expect a lot of credit for the accomplishments of his first term; Miller was in a much better position to claim and receive all the credit. At the same time, Patrick could not really attack an administration of which he had been a part. Patrick's strategy, therefore, involved picturing himself as the last remnant of MFD and reform-minded, rank-and-file leadership in the union and painting an optimistic but realistic view of the UMW's future. Patrick, like the other two candidates, endorsed the right-to-strike proposal. Whereas political necessity forced the other candidates to support this provision, Patrick had supported it well before election time. The most militant of the three, he stated that many of the wildcat problems could be solved "if union officers stood up for miners when they're right instead of ducking."[62]

Patrick's job as secretary-treasurer of the union forced him into a difficult position concerning the financial issues. Although he tried to defend the job he had done and convince the voters that the financial state of the union was good, he could not escape the well-publicized accounts of his difficulties in handling the dues system. In the end, he plainly suffered from the charges. Although his job responsibilities did not extend to the Welfare and Retirement Funds, he knew the dangers it faced. He attempted to make the voters aware of the

Funds' precarious position and, as Patterson had, warned of a cut in health benefits.[63]

Patrick's approach to contract negotiations was more solidly conceived. He associated himself with the strong aspects of the present contract and pledged to work to correct the weaknesses. Picturing himself as an experienced negotiator, Patrick stressed the role he had played in the 1974 negotiations. Patrick did not make unpracticable promises, but said he would work within the guidelines of the bargaining process, involving the rank and file to the greatest degree possible. He concentrated long and hard on this issue above all others.[64]

Patrick's campaign was broader than that of the other candidates and went well beyond the three issues described. He stressed other union programs and pledged to support and promote them. High on his list was a plan for organizing more coal miners, particularly in the western United States. This, Patrick stated, would be a high priority of his administration. He stressed the importance of education and political action and pledged to expand both programs within the union. Patrick also dwelled on the issue of leadership ability. Attempting to depict Miller as lacking any ability and desire to lead the union, he described the lack of administrative and decision-making ability on Miller's part that he had witnessed throughout the last administration.[65]

The election took place on June 14, 1977. Whereas in 1972 miners voted at a number of places near the mine site, such as the local union hall, firehall, social club, or at the mine site itself, voting in the 1977 election took place exclusively at the mine site. The bathhouse or other company building at the portal, preparation plant, or strip site, served as the polls. Thus, if a UMW member came to work, he came to the polls. This right was first secured during the 1974 negotiations and was meant to encourage more union members to participate in union elections by making the voting process almost effortless. Given the circumstances, the candidates predicted a heavy turnout for the June elections. They were wrong. Of the approximately 277,000 active and retired miners eligible to vote in 1977, only 138,840 or barely 50 percent actually did.[66]

Table 5   Results of the 1977 UMW Presidential Election

District	Miller	Patterson	Patrick
2 Central Pennsylvania	6,740	2,775	2,231
4 Western Pennsylvania	3,043	1,263	893
5 Western Pennsylvania	5,934	2,725	996
6 Ohio	4,539	1,995	4,843
11 Indiana	653	1,965	548
12 Illinois	1,736	4,779	6,424
14 Iowa, Missouri, Kansas	35	733	52
15 Colorado, New Mexico Montana, N. Dakota	384	1,094	963
17 Southern West Virginia	8,416	2,685	3,756
18 Western Canada	377	81	670
19 Central Kentucky, Tennessee	910	1,424	607
20 Alabama	1,070	4,395	1,438
21 Arkansas, Oklahoma, Texas	47	539	72
22 Utah, Arizona, Wyoming	616	1,030	752
23 Western Kentucky	2,715	4,246	656
25 Eastern Pennsylvania	2,122	2,922	1,031
26 Nova Scotia, Canada	1,439	222	285
28 Virginia	2,167	3,670	2,162
29 Southern West Virginia	6,057	4,364	3,295
30 Eastern Kentucky	1,113	3,482	1,015
31 Northern West Virginia	5,162	2,653	1,834
Totals	55,275	49,042	34,523

Source: *UMW Journal,* July 16–31, 1977, p. 12.

Although the election took place June 14, the international union's tellers did not announce the election results until early July. Survey polls conducted by various sources, however, relieved the suspense by announcing projected tallies that in retrospect proved surprisingly accurate. The tellers' results, announced July 4, showed that Miller had won reelection as UMW president by defeating Lee Roy Patterson by just 6,233 votes. Miller received 55,275 votes to Patterson's 49,042. Harry Patrick finished a somewhat distant third with 34,523. The other candidates on Miller's slate captured all thirteen remaining slots.[67]

The election results said a great deal about the state of the

UMW in 1977 and about the future of the union. First, less than 20 percent of the eligible UMW voters, or one out of five, voted for Arnold Miller. This constituted less than a mandate; when the UMW needed strong leadership to unify the union, 60 percent of those voting opposed the top officer.[68] Such a weak vote of confidence in the incumbent president could do little to settle the internal power struggle plaguing the union.

Among other significant figures are those showing that Miller came in third among young miners, age eighteen to thirty-five; Harry Patrick won the young miner's vote, with approximately 39 percent to Patterson's 32 percent. This was significant because of the increasingly young average age of the union's workforce. Miller did, however, carry the important retired miner's vote, a group that historically has supported the incumbent. Miller took about 40 percent of this group's vote, with Patterson winning 34 percent and Patrick only 20 percent.[69]

Geographically, Miller's strength lay in the heart of the coal-fields. Over 50 percent of all UMW members live in Pennsylvania and West Virginia. Miller gained his election victory in these states. Results show that Miller won over 60 percent of the vote in Pennsylvania and over 50 percent of the vote in the West Virginia coalfields. Patterson did well in his home territory of Kentucky, while Patrick's only victories came in the Ohio and Illinois coal regions.[70]

In the final analysis, Miller won the election because of his incumbency, strengthened by the accomplishments of his first administration. The 1974 contract, the bread and butter factor, appeared particularly important. Despite the publicity and bombardment of literature, many miners apparently stayed completely detached from the election throughout the campaign. A primary concern of those who voted was the contract under which they would work. Many miners thought the 1974 agreement was a good contract. They believed that if Miller did it once, he deserved a chance to do it again. A secondary consideration involved the restoration of democratic processes in many areas within the union, including district elections and democratic conventions.[71]

Early in the campaign, based on the nomination vote and

early surveys, Lee Roy Patterson appeared the favorite. Patterson's lead dwindled because of a number of factors. Foremost among them was Patrick's attack on Patterson's Steelworkers connection. If coal miners, particularly Appalachian coal miners, are anything, they are independent-minded, particularly about their union. For them, the UMW is a union of coal miners and only coal miners. They do not want other workers in the UMW, and they do not want the UMW in another union. The 1976 convention made this clear when it summarily voted down a proposal to look into readmittance to the AFL-CIO.[72] Patrick shrewdly parlayed an innocuous Patterson statement at a press conference and a contribution from USW leaders into a major campaign issue. Undoubtedly this issue, combined with Patterson's well-publicized alliance with Boyle and his role as the sower of disunity during the first Miller administration, lead to Patterson's downfall.

All things considered, Harry Patrick ran a strong race, even though he finished third. Patrick came virtually out of nowhere to win 25 percent of the vote. He particularly came on strong in the last three weeks of the race as indicated by a professional poll commissioned in mid-May that showed Patrick with only 16 percent of the vote. Thus in the three weeks before the June 14 election, Patrick increased his support a full 9 percent. He accomplished this mainly by an exhausting face-to-face electioneering effort in the closing weeks of the race. His late start and lack of name recognition, as well as the charges of UMW financial mismanagement, hurt Patrick badly. If Patrick had had a few more weeks, the results might have been different. Despite the loss, his strength among the young miners indicated Patrick, only forty-six years old, could have a promising future in UMW politics.[73]

The 1977 UMW international elections did not end with the closing of the polls and the counting of the ballots. Along with his many campaign protests, threats, and lawsuits, Lee Roy Patterson had vowed, if he lost, to contest the election on the grounds of ballot irregularities and to force a rerun. After a period of indecision, Patterson announced on June 26 that he would ask the union tellers and the IEB to set the election aside because the tellers had unfairly granted slate privileges to

Miller's and Patrick's tickets.[74] In July, the tellers dismissed Patterson's charges for lack of evidence and certified the election results.[75] Later in the month, on July 21, the IEB, which in earlier years had usually voted with Patterson, also denied Patterson's complaints and accepted the tellers' decisions.[76] In October 1977, the U.S. Department of Labor turned down Patterson's appeal, finalizing the election results of July 1977.[77] Miller was sworn in for a second term as UMW president on December 22, 1977.[78]

The election of June 1977 and the campaign war leading up to it were unique and important occurrences in the history of the UMW since the 1920s. More dramatically than any single event, the open and democratic election process demonstrated the progress the union had made toward becoming a more democratic labor organization. This process was the most important legacy left to the UMW by Jock Yablonski and MFD as a result of their struggles with the Boyle regime.

Unlike the 1969 election, which was overturned by the government on the basis of massive illegalities committed by the Boyle administration, the 1977 election was reviewed by the Department of Labor and found in compliance with federal law. Unlike the government-supervised election of 1972, the UMW employed its own internal constitutional mechanisms, based on the Department of Labor standards used previously, to police the 1977 election. The union tellers, elected by the membership, supervised the election, allocated space in the *Journal* equally among the three candidates, heard appeals, and tabulated the results. Perhaps even more than in 1972, the 1977 election was a wide-open affair, with the challengers pursuing maximum exposure for themselves, their positions, and their slates. The *Journal*, televised debates, and active bathhouse-to-bathhouse campaigning were common means employed to reach as many voters as possible. Candidates using their qualifications and positions to actively and vigorously court voters was a true sign of an open and democratic election.

The reform administration from 1972 to 1977 experienced some problems. The bitter politics that permeated all aspects of the international union led to firings, resignations, the stagnation of reform, and eventually to the disintegration of the administration itself. But during its five years, the first Miller administration was also responsible for many positive reforms and advances. Of these, the open and democratic elections of 1977 and the orderly transfer of power to a second, but different, Miller adminstration stands as perhaps its greatest achievement. Enduring the test of a serious, hard fought campaign, the union proved that democracy in the UMW had come a long way since 1972.

7 The Union in Crisis

THE Miller administration's first term officially ended December 22, 1977. It had, however, ceased to function long before that date. In the six months following the June 15 elections, neither Mike Trbovich nor Harry Patrick had any real duties or authority as UMW officers. According to one senior staff member, the vice president–elect Sam Church and the secretary-treasurer-elect Bill Esselstyn assumed many of Patrick's and Trbovich's functions during this period. On December 22, 1977, the Miller administration's second term officially began with the formal inauguration of its new officers. Before two hundred guests at the Capitol Hilton Hotel in Washington, D.C., Arnold Miller was sworn in for a second five-year term as UMW president. Sam Church and Bill Esselstyn were sworn in as the new vice president and secretary-treasurer. Miller did not invite their predecessors, Trbovich and Patrick, to the ceremony.[1]

The departures of the two former MFD leaders marked the end of the reform administration and possibly the end of the reform movement for a more democratic miners' union. Mike Trbovich left office at the age of fifty-seven, a man broken both physically and politically. Black lung and diabetes forced him into retirement when his term expired. Unable to work or to collect an officer's pension from the UMW, since under reformed requirements officials were required to serve ten years before they received a pension from the union, Trbovich's only sources of income reportedly were his miner's pension of $225 a month and monthly federal black lung benefits of $300.[2]

Harry Patrick initially indicated that he would return to the mines and bide his time until he could seek office once again. Speaking at his campaign headquarters in the Fairmont, West Virginia, Holiday Inn on election night in June 1977, Patrick said,

> I'm a coal miner first. I don't know anything else. Absolutely, I'll come back to Barrackville [W. Va.] to work. A man who negotiates a contract has to be prepared to work under it. It'll be a tough adjustment but I fully realized this when I started.[3]

Having left the mines for an office job and having moved from rural West Virginia to suburban Washington, D.C., Patrick had acquired a new life-style that he was reluctant to give up. In his own words, he had "learned to love quiche Lorraine and Grand Marnier."[4] After putting in one shift at his former mine to protect his pension, Patrick stated, "If there was any kind of other job offer that would come along, I'd do it."[5] Shortly afterwards, Patrick relinquished his membership in the UMW, and in all probability his political future in the union, and took a job as a regional director with ACTION, a federal social agency.[6] Patrick's departure left a void in the leadership of the progressive element of the UMW.

As a result of his defeat, Lee Roy Patterson, Miller's other major political nemesis, was also forced to give up union office. Because of his bid for the UMW presidency, Patterson had been unable to run for his seat on the IEB. After the election, Patterson indicated, like Patrick, that he would return to work in the mines. In September 1977, Patterson's term as IEB member from District 23 expired, and he returned to his old job as machine operator at a Caney Creek, Kentucky, strip mine. By doing so, Lee Roy Patterson retained his eligibility to run for UMW office in the future.

The second Miller administration faced an increasingly dissatisfied membership. Much of this dissension centered on the problems of the Welfare and Retirement Funds. With medical costs spiraling, the blanket coverage of the welfare fund card was a cherished possession of miners and their families. On June 14, 1977, only four days after the 1977 international elections, the UMWA Welfare and Retirement Funds mailed letters

115

to all Funds beneficiaries notifying them of a cut in medical benefits effective July 1. For the first time in the thirty-year history of the Funds, miners and their dependents would be required to share the cost of medical care. After July 1, the Funds required beneficiaries to pay "the first $250 in hospital bills each year and 40 percent of all doctor bills up to $250 each year."[7]

The cut was determined by unanimous vote of the Funds' trustees—industry representative C. W. Davis, union representative Harry Huge, and neutral member Paul R. Dean. The rationale for the cut was that the Funds' income, which was based on royalties from each ton of coal produced, could not cover the cost of the benefits at their present level. The coal industry blamed production lost in unauthorized work stoppages for the shortfall, claiming wildcats had cost the Funds $81.2 million during the 1974 contract. Production losses from severe winter weather were held responsible for the loss of an additional $20 million in employer contributions. Inflation-fed increases in medical costs amplified the Funds' loss of expected income. Miners blamed inflation and bad weather for being as responsible as wildcat strikes for the Funds' precarious financial situation and accused the operators of forcing the cut by refusing to allow the redistribution of money within the Funds. Miners, as well as sources close to the Funds' administration, cited mismanagement of the program as an additional factor responsible for the crisis.[8]

Whatever its causes, the erosion of this blanket medical coverage was a tremendous blow to the UMW membership. Reaction was intensified when this shattering news hit only four days after the end of a campaign in which Miller had defended the stability of the Funds, while rival Harry Patrick charged a cut was imminent. Patrick later told an IEB meeting that he had proof the decision to cut coverage had been made June 9, five days before the elections. He implied that the Funds' union representative, Harry Huge, a Miller supporter who had donated a thousand dollars to the incumbent president's campaign, had kept the action secret to benefit Miller's election bid.[9]

On June 18, scattered strikes protesting the cutback developed in the eastern coalfields.[10] By June 21, thirteen thousand miners had walked off the job in West Virginia alone.[11] Spread by roving pickets the protest walkout grew steadily over several weeks despite the condemnation of the international union. By the seventh week, every mine in the state of West Virginia was shut down, and more than eighty thousand miners in the eastern coalfield states had walked out.[12] The miners eventually drifted back to work twelve weeks after the strike had begun.[13] Though the strike itself accomplished little, it had sullied both Miller's old and new administrations and left a large segment of the rank and file in an adversarial position to the union's leadership. In addition, the wildcats over the Funds had significance for the upcoming contract negotiations as it underscored UMW members' vital concern for the health benefits issue.

The most important challenge facing Arnold Miller and his second administration was the negotiation of a new contract. Having failed to get the operators to reopen the contract in July and renegotiate the health provisions, Miller faced a December 6, 1977, contract expiration date. Talks for the new agreement formally opened October 6 at the Capitol Hilton Hotel in Washington, D.C. After two months of bargaining with the Bituminous Coal Operators Association, the 1974 contract expired, and 180,000 coal miners, following the UMW tradition of no contract, no work, walked out. At the time of the strike, negotiators for the union and for the BCOA were still far apart. As expected, the coal operators had come to the bargaining table better prepared and less generous than in 1974. Miller came to the table unprepared, without adequate support staff, and tied by campaign pledges to demands viewed by the operators as impossible to grant. The result was inevitable.

The union's new administration had no alternative but to take a long strike and attempt to narrow the gap at the table by softening the hard stances of both the BCOA and its own membership. UMW members had high expectations for the new contract. They had delineated their priorities in the collective bargaining report of the 1976 convention. Topping the list of contract demands was a provision ensuring the right to strike at the local level. The report also directed the UMW bargaining team to seek a substantial wage increase; more vacation, sick,

117

and personal days; graduated vacations; a change in the seniority system; the six-hour day; and other items.[14]

The right-to-strike issue was a very emotional, highly politicized issue that was bound to be a stumbling block in negotiations. Unlike most contemporary collective bargaining agreements, modern UMW contracts have lacked no-strike provisions. A United States Supreme Court decision in the Boys Market case of 1970, however, ruled that every contract containing an arbitration clause, as the UMW contract did, also contained an implied no-strike pledge.[15] This made all strikes during the duration of a contract illegal. It also allowed coal operators to obtain court orders enjoining these strikes, something that occurred with regularity. The wildcat strikes continued regardless, to the detriment of both miners and mine-owners.

The right-to-strike proposal was the union's solution to the problem. The UMW proposed that when a local dispute arose that could not be settled in the grievance procedure, the local union would vote whether to arbitrate the dispute or to strike. The scheme included several safeguards. For an issue to be considered, it would have to be "of such a magnitude as to affect all, or a large number of the members working at an affected mine." No vote could be scheduled until local officers met and gave their approval. A seventy-two hour cooling-off period would then be necessary before a strike vote could be held. After this cooling-off period, a meeting could be scheduled at which a secret ballot vote would be taken. Any strike required the approval of a majority of all miners working at a particular mine.[16]

The UMW saw this as a means of countering management's use of arbitration as a tactical weapon. By putting the decision of whether to arbitrate or to strike in the miners' hands, coal operators would no longer be able to delay dealing with problems by forcing issues to the costly, time-consuming arbitration level. The union also contended that it would help solve the problem of roving pickets spreading wildcats from mine to mine and insisted that the process would eventually lead to improved labor-management relations. The industry did not agree. Referring to the right-to-strike proposal, one industry source close to the 1977–78 negotiations stated, "We never gave the UMWA proposal a serious hearing."[17] Coal management believed that legitimizing strikes during a contract would not bring stability to the industry. James R. Thomas II, head of the West Virginia Coal Association, took the position that the right to strike would "mean more instability. A contract without labor peace is no contract at all."[18]

The stalemate was further complicated by Miller's political commitment to the right to strike. The three candidates in the 1977 UMW election had fallen over each other in their rush to support this issue; strong membership sentiment demanded the right to strike. Joseph P. Brennan, BCOA president, reportedly told the operators that Miller would not endorse a contract for membership ratification unless it contained a right-to-strike clause.[19] Thus, Miller was placed in the difficult position of convincing the BCOA to accept a proposition that was anathema to them, or convincing his membership that the provision was impossible to win. In many respects, this process of persuasion was what the long strike of 1977–78 was about.

The stalemate on the right-to-strike issue was made complete by the industry's decision to take a hard line in negotiations on the wildcat problem. Brennan announced, before the opening of talks, that the BCOA was determined to reclaim "the right to operate our mines during a contract term without the constant debilitating imprint of the wildcat."[20] The BCOA followed this up in negotiations by including a strong measure dealing with labor stability in its initial proposals. Going farther than the traditional labor agreement no-strike pledge, the operators proposed a provision to dock the pay of striking miners 40 percent, on their return to work, for each day they stayed off the job in an illegal work stoppage. This penalty fee would be passed on to the UMWA Welfare and Retirement Funds. As negotiations progressed, the BCOA proposed additional disciplinary measures for miners involved in wildcat strikes, including the absolute right to discharge those active in fomenting unauthorized work stoppages; they proposed, in addition, that passive participants in wildcats, those refusing to cross a picket line, could be suspended for thirty days without pay. Under these proposed contract provisions, an arbitrator could not modify the penalty imposed in either of these cases if guilt were sustained. The operators thought this system would return control of the work force to them and bring stability to the coal industry, something they believed was badly needed if coal was to assume a strong role in the nation's energy picture. Obviously, the two parties' positions were at opposite poles.[21]

The issue of labor stability was not the only extremely difficult issue that had to be resolved in negotiations. Just as important and difficult was the status of the Welfare and Retirement Funds, specifically the health benefits question. The Funds' problems and subsequent benefits cuts came to light only months before talks began, and thus proposals to deal with the problems were not mandated by the convention. The wildcats protesting the cutbacks the preceding summer, however, marked the health benefits issue as a top bargaining priority. Miller, from the beginning, took the position that the union would not move forward in negotiations until the industry agreed to cancel the cuts completely and restore health services under the royalty-financed Funds. Three weeks into the talks Miller even broke off bargaining completely because of a deadlock on the issue. He said, "Whenever the BCOA is willing to respond in a constructive manner on the question of the Funds, we will be ready to resume negotiations."[22]

Miller's emphasis on this issue seemed to reflect the sentiments of the rank-and-file miner in the coalfields. The attitude of Chester Shadrick of Oceana, West Virginia, seemed typical: "I'm not looking for a high wage, I'm looking for benefits. The only reason I'm working in the mines is to get that (health benefits) card."[23] Referring to the health benefits enjoyed before the cutback, another miner expressed his concern and frustration: "The men want the whole damn thing back. And they just hate to bargain for something they've had for years."[24]

Industry negotiators, however, were reluctant to discuss the issue as a precondition to other issues. From the BCOA's point of view, the Funds–health benefits issue was tied very closely to the industry's number-one bargaining concern—labor stability. Since the union had made clear that its goal was to retain the present royalty-financed benefits system, the operators were very reluctant to even discuss the issue until they could get a definite feeling for how far the UMW was willing to go in cracking down on the wildcat problem. The BCOA seemed to believe that they could not even discuss the Funds' financial situation, including the level of royalties and benefits, until they had some guarantee of labor stability for the next three years. Ideally, if the BCOA could win agreement on its proposal to force the miners to contribute to the Funds in the form of fines for unauthorized walkouts, the industry would be in a much more advantageous position to discuss the Funds question. Responsibility for the Funds' finances would then, to some degree, be jointly shared by the miners and the operators. Again, the scene was set for a long impasse.

By the December 6 strike deadline, after two months of bargaining, very little progress had been made. Only the two major issues, labor stability and health benefits, had been seriously discussed, and there had been very little movement on either issue by either side. Despite some suggestions by Arnold Miller that the contract deadline be extended, coal miners at mines all across America walked off the job at 12:01 a.m., December 6.[25]

From the October 6 opening of negotiations through the December 6 deadline, the UMW negotiating team experienced problems, separate from the substantive bargaining issues, that had considerable effect on the bargaining process. One problem was the state of readiness of the UMW for nationwide bargaining with the coal industry. A second significant problem was the effectiveness of the union's chief negotiator, Arnold Miller.

The 1974 negotiations had been a team effort. At that time the UMW officers had tremendous support and assistance from talented union staffers like lawyers Rick Bank and Chip Yablonski, research director Tom Bethell, and economists Tom Woodruff and Don Pierce. Preparations for negotiations were detailed, extensive, and sophisticated. When talks began in 1974, UMW negotiators presented the BCOA with an inch-thick set of demands and background data explaining and supporting the demands. Given the history of coal industry bargaining before 1974, the industry was immediately placed on the defensive.

In 1977, the first meeting of the negotiating teams created a different scene. When bargaining began on October 7, Miller reportedly failed to present even a list of demands and distributed only a three-page list of bargaining goals to the press. Most of the meeting consisted of a slide presentation of industry economics, with BCOA president Brennan doing the talking. A major coalfield newspaper ran a large headline after the first day of talks declaring "Coal Talks Stalled, Union Isn't Ready."[26] If the coal industry wanted the miners' union on the defensive in 1977, it had succeeded.

There were several reasons for this lack of preparation and why it may have been damaging. Of the international officers and top staff who had negotiated the 1974 contract, only Arnold Miller remained. Mike Trbovich and Harry Patrick, although technically in office through December 1977, were lame ducks and were not involved in the 1977 talks. The staff members involved in 1974 had resigned or been fired; many of them had never been replaced. Elected in the June elections, Sam Church and Bill Esselstyn had little, if any, bargaining experience at the national level and, although they had already begun to assume responsibility, they would not be installed as officers until December. Having survived a hotly contested election just four months earlier, as well as a couple years of internecine strife, Miller had neither the time or resources to prepare for bargaining on October 6.

To help compensate for these weaknesses, Miller retained outside consultants to assist in contract talks. In September, he named Ronald G. Nathan, special counsel and bargaining coordinator, and Philip J. Mause, special counsel for economic issues. Both were from the Washington, D.C., law firm of Nathan, Mause, and Thorpe. The economic research firm of Ruttenberg, Friedman, Kilgallon, Gutchess, and Associates and communications and public relations specialists Maurer, Fleisher, Zon, and Anderson, were also hired in September.[27] Other minor support staff were retained to work on negotiations. For the most part, this support staff was not hired in time to really prepare for the opening of negotiations, and undoubtedly, the slow start caused the UMW and the BCOA to lose valuable bargaining time. Reports also indicated that the hiring of some of these consultants and staffers was not entirely the union's idea. The Federal Mediation and Conciliation Service (FMCS), a government dispute settlement agency, reportedly lined up some of this assistance in an effort to aid the negotiations process. A government agency helping a union prepare itself for contract talks was a further indication of the lack of organization and preparation within the UMW.[28]

Primary responsibility for a union's performance at the bargaining table falls with the union's chief negotiator. In 1977, Arnold Miller's effectiveness as head of the UMW's bargaining team was called into question by significant elements of both the union and the industry. Problems arose not only from Miller's apparent lack of preparation, organization, and experience but also from his unpredictable and inconstant personality. Much of the criticism from within the UMW stemmed from the shroud of secrecy Miller hung over the talks. Officials at every level of the union complained of a widespread lack of knowledge about the status and progress of negotiations throughout the six-month period. Whether the blackout was intentional or accidental, it contributed to the spread of rumors and misinformation that in turn led to increased dissension and criticism.[29]

Miller's inaccessibility also contributed to the confusion that surrounded negotiations. As negotiations wore on, Miller's attendance at bargaining sessions became sporadic. During critical periods in the talks Miller was nowhere to be found. Reports began to appear alleging that for days on end his own office aides had no idea where he was. Miller was said to be spending more and more of his time at the Heart O'Town motel in Charleston, West Virginia, despite his demand for around-the-clock bargaining. Stories circulated of Miller's turning up at a Georgetown party while union and industry representatives worked at the table until the early hours of the morning. At one point the UMW president reportedly drove around the Washington, D. C., beltway while talks were in progress, apparently in an effort to escape the building pressure.[30]

This erratic behavior had been developing since late in his first term when Miller, as one former aide put it, "began seeking an enemy under every bed."[31] Miller became increasingly suspicious and isolated, and his circle of confidantes became ever smaller as he attempted to insulate himself from the increasing opposition and dissension within the UMW. By early 1978, the pressure of bargaining had hastened this process. One veteran labor observer reported, "He's almost become a recluse. You just never see him anymore."[32] Certainly Arnold Miller appeared to feel surrounded and cut off from any base of support. This feeling seemed to deepen as bargaining progressed and the Bargaining Council and membership rejected Miller-endorsed contracts.

This "bunker" mentality, first reported by Harry Patrick near the end of Miller's first term, manifested itself in other ways. During negotiations, Miller began carrying a gun tucked in his belt under his necktie after he received several death threats. He was also usually accompanied by a couple union staffers, hired as "international representatives," but whose main responsibility apparently was to be bodyguards to the president. At one point Miller told reporters, "I've been receiving very serious personal threats on my life. I've received information that someone is going to Chicago to hire a professional to kill me. I can handle most things, but if someone hires a professional, they're going to get you."[33] All in all, Miller's circle-the-wagons state of mind was strangely reminiscent of Tony Boyle's outlook when his administration was under siege. It was, without question, a hinderance, if not a major obstacle, during the contract talks of 1977–78.

Like their counterparts in the union, industry representatives voiced their unhappiness with Miller's performance as the UMW's chief negotiator. Aside from the normal disagreement over substantive issues, industry bargainers attacked Miller on a more personal level, charging that Miller was "unpredictable" and "slow to grasp technical issues."[34] They contended that he was inconsistent and changed his position on issues overnight. In short, they argued that Miller was an impediment to progress at the bargaining table. At one point Joseph Brennan, the leader of the BCOA bargaining team, offered to step down from his position as chief industry bargainer if Miller would hand the bargaining chores over to someone else on the union side. There were also reports of efforts by UMW representatives and the Federal Mediation and Conciliation Service to remove Miller from the union's negotiating team.[35] Even given the usual give-and-take of negotiations, these were unusual developments. Miller's performance, and the dissatisfaction of both union and industry officials with it, undoubtedly had a substantial effect on the outcome of bargaining.

One group that had virtually no influence on the bargaining process but was raised to importance by the coalfield press was the radical left wing. Specifically, attention was focused on the Miners' Right-to-Strike Committee (MRSC), a militant rank-and-file group with only a handful of members. By simultaneously picturing this group as the standard-bearer for the contractual right-to-strike issue and "revealing" that some of their members had ties to a communist splinter group, the Revolutionary Communist Party, U.S.A., the press inspired red-baiting that clouded the issues and divided the union membership. The MRSC was, and is, an insignificant organization that sometimes attracted more reporters than miners to its rallies. By printing numerous feature articles and editorials spotlighting coalfield radicals and blaming the MRSC for past and present troubles, including bargaining problems, the press further inflamed and confused an already volatile and potentially violent situation.[36] Extraneous and secondary issues like this, and like the internal political problems of the UMW, played important roles in the 1977–78 contract negotiations.

Talks continued after the December 6 shutdown, with the focus of negotiations remaining the right-to-strike, or labor stability, issue and the health benefits issue. Information about the talks was closely guarded, but it was apparent that progress was slow. Negotiations broke down for the third time on December 30 when the BCOA representatives walked out of the talks upon the UMW's presentation of a proposal for complete restoration of the Funds. The union angered the operators by refusing to tie the benefits issue to some kind of proposal for labor stability.[37]

Talks resumed on January 12, the sixth week of the strike. Union negotiators again angered the operators by reintroducing the right-to-strike provision, an issue the BCOA thought they had taken off the table.[38] Twelve days later on January 24, the industry negotiators once again walked out. Contributing to this breakdown was the occurrence of some secret, high-level negotiations between a senior UMW aide and a small industry group.[39] The failure of these talks, and the infighting that followed within both the UMW and the BCOA bargaining teams, suggested that internal differences on both sides were a significant impediment to settlement.

When the two sides returned to the bargaining table in late January, they made considerable progress. By February 6, union and industry negotiators reached a tentative settlement. The agreement provided for a wage increase of $2.35 an hour over three years with the total economic package amounting to a nearly 37 percent increase over the 1974 contract. The crucial parts of the settlement, however, were the health benefits and labor stability provisions. The health benefits clause provided for a fundamental change in the amount of benefits provided and in the manner the industry would provide them. The proposed agreement would have replaced the jointly administered, industry-financed health fund with company-by-company commercial insurance plans, and would have instituted, in place of the expired contract's free medical care, a maximum deductible fee plan, with deductions of $700 for nonparticipating hospitals and $325 for participating hospitals.[40]

It was significant that the provision dealing with the wildcat strike problem was widely reported in the media as the "labor-stability" provision and not as the "right-to-strike" provision. The proposed agreement made it clear that the union had been unable to win any kind of language legitimizing walkouts during the course of the agreement. The labor stability clause came down hard on such strikes by requiring miners engaged in wildcats to "reimburse" the benefit funds for retired miners $20 a day for up to ten days on strike. It also allowed employers to fire miners who led unauthorized walkouts and to suspend without pay for up to thirty days miners who honored the picket line.[41]

The health benefits and labor stability provisions came under sharp criticism by many in the union. This dissatisfaction was reflected when the Bargaining Council, the first step in the UMW's contract ratification process, rejected the proposal by a thirty-to-six vote.[42] Despite Arnold Miller's assertion that ". . . 90

percent of our industry wanted to work and . . . would have accepted this contract," the vote seemed to reflect the feelings of many rank-and-file miners in the coalfields.[43] The contract's strong rejection ensured the continuation of the strike, which was already seventy days old.

On February 15, at President Jimmy Carter's personal request, contract talks resumed at the White House. The next day they moved to the Department of Labor. With President Carter raising the possibility of seeking a Taft-Hartley injunction against the strike and with Secretary of Labor Ray Marshall personally supervising the talks, pressure for a settlement was greatly increasing. After two days of marathon bargaining under the government's watchful eye, a new proposal, quite similar to the previously rejected pact, was presented to the Bargaining Council. The council, in an unofficial vote, rejected it thirty-three to three.[44]

In the next week, the president stepped up his campaign to achieve a settlement. During that time the UMW negotiators rejected a BCOA proposal to submit the dispute to binding arbitration if the miners would return to work and accepted a tentative agreement with a non-BCOA coal company, Pittsburg and Midway Coal.[45] The latter occurrence had considerable significance because its terms set, in the eyes of many UMW officials, a pattern for settlement of the nationwide conflict.

On February 25, the coal industry and the UMW reached yet another tentative settlement based largely on the Pittsburg and Midway agreement. The wage package was similar to the February 6 settlement, an increase of $2.40 over three years or a little over 37 percent in the total package, although the February 25 proposal did provide for a cost-of-living adjustment in the second and third years. The health benefits provision was also somewhat similar to the earlier settlement. Health benefits would be provided by private insurance plans on a company-by-company basis. The new plan would impose the payment of a $700 deductible on UMW members.[46]

The labor stability language, however, was drastically changed from the previous agreement. Industry proposals to fire or fine miners participating in unauthorized work stoppages, including those that honored picket lines, were dropped; management's right to discharge or discipline anyone who instigated wildcat strikes, however, was retained. The UMW's proposed right to strike had been dropped earlier in negotiations.[47]

The Bargaining Council was not asked to vote on this proposed contract since it had previously approved the Pittsburg and Midway agreement, on which it was based, by a twenty-five to thirteen vote. Instead, the union's leadership moved quickly to begin the membership ratification process. Miller and other top UMW officials decided not to leave the approval of this proposed contract to chance and began a vigorous campaign to sell the contract. Union officials spent $40,000 to whip up support for ratification of the agreement. Country singer Johnny Paycheck was recruited to push the proposal by singing a few lines from the popular song "Spread the Good News Around" in radio ads. UMW international and district officers fanned out through the coalfields to praise the agreement, both in person and over nine television and fifty radio stations.[48] This hard sell was met with disapproval by many union members. "If this contract is such a hot deal it would sell itself. But it can't," was the comment of miner Howard White of Benham, Kentucky.[49] White was not alone in his opposition.

Dissatisfaction was evident in the coalfields. The media had a field day reporting on protest rallies, contract burnings, and rowdiness at union meetings called to explain the proposal. The UMW membership made its feelings clear on March 5 when it rejected the proposed settlement by a two-to-one margin.[50]

This rejection of a possible settlement to the ninety-day coal strike elicited a strong reaction from the public and President Carter. As coal stocks fell to critical levels and schools began to close or turn their heat down drastically, as violence against nonunion miners, coal truckers, and company property increased, so did opposition to the strike among the American public. Polls showed a sharp decline in the number of individuals who supported the strike, and editorials in newspapers from the *Washington Post* to the *Bluefield* (West Virginia) *Daily Telegraph* almost unanimously blasted the obstinance of the mine workers.[51] At the same time, President Carter intensified his involvement in the dispute the day after the vote by calling for a Taft-Hartley injunction. This strong action, although supported by the public, met with strong opposition from UMW miners. When a temporary back-to-work order was issued by a U.S. district court on March 10, the order was largely ignored.[52] The government's intervention in the strike only escalated tensions and increased the chance of violent confrontation on a larger scale.

Fortunately, this confrontation never materialized. The UMW and the BCOA resumed negotiations, and on March 14 they once again reached a tentative agreement.[53] The following day, March 15, the Bargaining Council approved the pact by a twenty-two to seventeen vote.[54] Relieved of the pressure of the Taft-Hartley injunction when a Washington judge denied the government's request for a continuance of the original back-to-work order, the union leadership took a more low-key approach to the promotion of the latest agreement.[55] When the official ratification vote was held March 24, UMW miners accepted the proposed contract by a vote of 58,802 to 44,457 or 57 to 43 percent.[56] During the week of March 27, UMW miners returned to the mines, marking an end to the 110-day strike, the longest in UMW history.

In the weeks and months following the strike, miners, the press, and the public speculated about what the strike had accomplished. Had the mine workers "won"? Had the gains justified the losses and sacrifices of a record strike? Or had the miners simply been beaten, worn down by the hard line of the coal operators and the weakness and ineptitude of their own leadership? Without question, the final pact negotiated by union and industry bargainers did include significant concessions from the BCOA, many of which were not included in the previous pacts rejected by the Bargaining Council and the membership.

From the union's point of view, perhaps the biggest achievement was keeping the industry from writing any language into the contract dealing with the labor stability issue. BCOA demands for the contractual right to fire, fine, or discipline miners instigating a strike, picketing a mine, or refusing to cross a picket line, which had been a high priority issue for the industry, were dropped. The resolution of the labor stability issue, however, was not really a victory for the union, because a broad arbitration precedent allowing operators to discharge wildcat strike leaders remained intact, and the UMW's high priority demand for the right to strike had also been dropped.[57]

In addition to the labor stability question, the union did convince the BCOA to moderate its proposals on revamping the health benefits plan. While the union bargainers could not keep the free medical care miners had enjoyed under the UMW Funds for thirty years and were forced to agree to the Funds' replacement with company-by-company private insurance plans, the union did win a reduction of the maximum deductibles UMW members would have to pay for medical care in the future from $700 in the February 7 pact to $200 in the ratified contract. The new contract also provided eye care coverage for the first time, as well as improved sickness and accident benefits.[58]

The wage offer in the approved agreement was similar to those made in the rejected agreements. Miners' wages would increase $2.40 an hour over three years, or a little more than 37 percent. As in the other key areas, the UMW's accomplishments here were watered down by concessions to the industry. Specifically, the operators won the right to establish production incentive programs at mines where miners voted their approval. By winning this limited provision on incentives, the BCOA forced the union to accept something it had long opposed on the basis that the rush to production bonuses would lead to sacrifices in safety.[59]

While the UMW won other concessions, including an increase of twenty-five dollars a month for pensioners who retired before January 1, 1976, an expansion of and increase in life insurance benefits, and two additional floating vacation days, very few of the demands spelled out at the 1976 convention were included in the new agreement. The union's role in the 1977–78 negotiations, and throughout the 110-day strike, had been largely defensive. The coal operators had vigorously pushed their demands, and the union had fought hard to resist. Some considered this resistance to industry takeaways a victory. Arnold Miller assessed the settlement this way: "I don't think we gained all that much, but we kept what we had." Many in the union were not satisfied with this. "I think the member-ship of the UMW has been forced to accept what was left of the Last Supper," said John Mendoz, a miner from Chapmanville, West Virginia. "Miller went to the bargaining table and he picked up the crumbs the operators left and brought them to the mineworkers as a contract."[60] Whether the successful ratifi-cation vote reflected support for the contract or desperation brought on by the 110-day strike was not clear. What was clear was that the 1977–78 negotiations and strike had further frac-tionalized an already divided union.

The less than satisfactory agreement and the three rejections of Miller-endorsed settlements, two by the Bargaining Council and one by the membership, brought Miller's credibility and that of his new administration crashing to the ground. The words of a country and western song, popular in the coalfields after the strike, were indicative of the feelings of at least some miners toward their leadership:

When Miller signed *their* contract
He might as well 'been on their side.
And the union said that's all she wrote—
Get on your horse and ride.[61]

The trauma of the election of 1977 and the negotiations and strike of 1977–78 were accompanied by definite changes in the style and actions of Arnold Miller and his administration. The idealism and zeal with which the first administration pursued democratic reform were gone, seemingly supplanted by seeds of the cynicism and inertia that had characterized the adminis-tration MFD replaced. One striking symbol of this change was the return of luxury cars for officer use. Among the first ac-tions of the reform administration in 1973 was the sale of Ca-dillac limousines used by the Boyle administration. Arnold Miller had made a dramatic production of his end-of-an-era Cadillac sale, at the time stating the cars were one of the rea-sons you "couldn't tell the union from the coal companies."[62] As late as May 1977, Miller campaign material in the *UMW Journal* asked, "Why is the 1974 contract the best in our his-tory? Because it wasn't written by leaders who ride around in fancy limousines."[63] Six months later, in December 1977, the

UMW leased a new, nine-passenger Cadillac limousine, which according to Miller would allow UMW officers to travel in "proper dignity."[64] When asked about the incongruence of this and his actions in 1973, the UMW president's office had "no comment."[65]

There were more important symptoms of a change in attitude on the part of the union's leadership. Miller's distance from the membership increased. This had been dramatized by confrontations with rank-and-file miners who had come to union headquarters during the strike to demonstrate. Miller caused several of these ugly situations by refusing to meet with members who had come long distances to air their views.[66] During the course of bargaining, he had avoided irate miners, the press, and sometimes even the negotiating table itself—at a time when the union needed a strong, visible leader. He did not act like the same leader who had run on a platform stressing the need for responsive and accessible leadership.

Several other reforms that Miller had pursued in his early years in office were dropped or altered by his second administration. Education was to have been given a high priority in building the union and in helping its officers and members deal more effectively with their problems. This increased emphasis was mandated by convention resolution and constitutional provision, and some initial progress had been made in developing pilot educational programs in several areas. The research department was very active during Miller's first term, providing assistance and backup to miners, union officers, and other international departments in many areas, including safety, housing, legislation, economic issues, and contract problems. By the end of Miller's first administration, the UMW education and research departments were all but nonexistent, and the early education programs had been mothballed.

A very visible gauge of the changes in style and substance of Miller's leadership through the years has been the *UMW Journal*. Don Stillman, the first UMW editor under Miller, and Matt Witt, his successor, were largely responsible for transforming the paper from a sycophantic house organ to a democratic publication used to inform the members and to serve as a forum for the rank and file. This was accomplished during the reform administration's first term with the support and approval of Miller. Toward the end of his first term, Miller's enthusiasm for an open and democratic *Journal* waned. As Witt explained,

> His top aide began to censor letters to the editor and ordered publication of a photograph and puff piece promoting a pro-Miller executive-board member facing a tough reelection fight. Miller also decided that the coverage of the final months of the 1977 contract talks would no longer be as open as in 1974.
>
> Instead, the *Journal* offered material on bargaining prepared by an outside public-relations concern; it emphasized the qualifications of union negotiators and featured a photograph of Miller on the average of one for each page. After nearly five years in which no national or district officer was pictured on a *Journal* cover, Miller himself became a regular, appearing on the front of three of the five issues from October 1977 to February 1978.[67]

After Witt's resignation in October 1977, the quality of the publication diminished noticeably. The "Contract Education" and "Rank and File Speaks" columns and the critical analysis of controversial issues facing miners were replaced by items reminiscent of Tony Boyle's *Journal*, "newsy" stories of poor quality and little worth. Witt was followed by a succession of three editors, each resigning after brief tenures. In early 1980, the UMW leadership appointed its sixth *Journal* editor in eight years.

Miller became increasingly impatient with his own reforms in other areas as well. After negotiations had ended, Miller announced that at the next convention he would seek to abolish the Bargaining Council, a reform he had supported in 1973 to ensure more involvement of the membership in the bargaining process.[68] The location of the next convention was another issue on which Miller had come full circle since his MFD days. One of Miller's major campaign issues while running on the MFD ticket in 1972 was that Boyle had held the previous two UMW conventions in cities outside the main eastern coalfields—Bal Harbour, Florida, in 1964 and Denver, Colorado, in 1968; Miller contended that these locations isolated the proceedings from the membership while costing the union thousands of dollars in unnecessary travel expense. In August 1978 he announced that the next UMW convention would be held in Miami, Florida, in late September 1979.[69] Then, because of Florida's failure to pass the Equal Rights Amendment, the union decided to switch the site of the upcoming convention. In June 1979, Miller announced that the 1979 UMW convention would be held December 10 to December 20 in Denver, Colorado.[70]

A final area in which there appeared to be some regression was in the amount of total compensation received by the international officers. As table 6 indicates, between 1973 and 1979, there was a marked increase in the amount of money UMW officers received in both salaries and expenses. Although the UMW constitution still sets the salaries of the international president, vice president, and secretary-treasurer at $35,000, $30,000, and $30,000, respectively, it also empowers the IEB to ". . . increase the salaries of officers and employees in the same percentage as the increase in the basic wage."[71] The wage increases negotiated in 1974 and 1978 account for most of the increase in officers' salaries. In 1974 the constitutional provision that UMW officers not be paid during an authorized strike accounted for the drop in salaries that year. Suspensions, leaves without pay, and other miscellaneous factors accounted for the fluctuations in other years.

Given the wage increases won by the administration and the inflation occurring during those years, the salary increases received by UMW international officers from 1973 to 1979 do not seem unreasonable. Yet, the increases in expenses of all three officers, particularly in recent years, appears to be another story. In the first year of Miller's initial term, the expenses of all three officers ranged from $3,000 to $4,000 each. In 1979, officers' expenses ranged from Miller's $22,577 to Esselstyn's $25,270. From 1973 to 1979, the UMW president's expenses rose 469 percent, the vice president's expenses rose 651 percent, and the secretary-treasurer's expenses increased a dramatic 681 percent.[72] Even given the rapid rise in travel costs, hotel bills, and food prices, these increases seem high. In light of Miller's and MFD's criticism of the lavish expense accounts of the Boyle administration, it is clear that a definite change in

Table 6   Salaries and Expenses of UMW International
               Officers, 1973–79

	President	Vice President	Secretary-Treasurer
1973	Miller	Trbovich	Patrick
Salary	36,284.00	31,101.00	31,105.00
Expenses	3,967.00	3,049.00	3,235.00
1974	Miller	Trbovich	Patrick
Salary	32,549.00	29,290.00	29,163.00
Expenses	3,215.00	1,792.00	2,221.00
1975	Miller	Trbovich	Patrick
Salary	45,309.00	35,469.00	35,676.00
Expenses	3,390.00	3,308.00	3,753.00
1976	Miller	Trbovich	Patrick
Salary	45,881.00	33,855.00	37,234.00
Expenses	20,593.00	8,281.00	10,175.00
1977	Miller	Trbovich	Patrick
Salary	40,384.00	29,835.00	34,852.00
Expenses	14,895.00	5,336.00	7,481.00
1978	Miller	Church	Esselstyn
Salary	41,892.00	36,815.00	36,706.00
Expenses	14,339.00	14,668.00	13,748.00
1979	Miller	Church	Esselstyn
Salary	42,569.00	33,289.00	37,495.00
Expenses	22,577.00	22,909.00	25,270.00

Source: LM-2 reports filed with the Labor-Management Services Administration, U.S. Department of Labor

attitude on the part of Arnold Miller and his administration had occurred.[73]

These changes in the Miller administration and the traumatic events of the early days of his second term alienated and estranged much of the union's membership. In the midst of the 1977–78 strike, the rank and file began to translate their distrust and dissatisfaction into action. On several occasions during the walkout, hundreds of miners traveled to UMW headquarters in Washington to protest settlements, at one point taking over the building in an act of defiance.[74] Activists also

135

pursued constitutional means to influence and possibly even replace the union's leadership. In mid-February 1978, rank and file members launched a recall campaign that grew after the strike settlement. By mid-July, thirty-one thousand miners had signed petitions asking for Miller's firing.[75] Although the recall effort needed only ten thousand signatures to instigate proceedings against the president, Miller's supporters on the IEB quashed the movement on a constitutional technicality.[76]

Arnold Miller was no longer a reformer, and the administration he led was no longer pursuing significant democratic change within the union. Reform had stagnated and, in some cases, been reversed. The leader of the 1972 movement for a more democratic UMW apparently believed that the reform of the miners' union had gone far enough. In some cases, as he stated in December 1978, they had gone "too far."[77]

Although he had publicly announced his intention to take measures to repeal or moderate some of his reforms, Miller never had the opportunity. Four days after signing the 1978 labor agreement with the BCOA, Miller suffered a slight stroke in Miami, Florida.[78] Two weeks later, while recuperating in the hospital, he was stricken with a mild heart attack.[79] Miller had a history of medical problems, including pneumoconiosis, arthritis, and the effects of head and face injuries sustained in World War II. In addition to these problems he had been hospitalized for exhaustion and chest pains. Only fifty-five years old in 1978, Arnold Miller looked and moved like a much older man. In March 1979, he again suffered heart problems, and in November 1979 he was hospitalized with more severe cardiac trouble.[80] Plagued by ill health and buffeted by political infighting, Miller resigned as president of the UMW on November 16, 1979. Vice president Sam Church was sworn into office as president the same day.[81]

While Sam Church's rise to the top position in the mine workers union was not as mercurial as Arnold Miller's, it was uncommonly rapid. Born in Matewan, West Virginia, in 1936, the son of a disabled coal miner, Church began work as an electrician in a southwestern Virginia mine at the age of twenty-nine. He spent only eight years in the mines, during which time he served in several local union offices, including mine committeeman, safety committeeman, financial secretary, and local president. During this period, he was a strong backer of UMW president Tony Boyle and actively supported him in his reelection bid against Miller in 1972. "I worked real hard for Boyle," Church has said. "I just thought he was the right man."[82] Elected as a field representative for District 28 in 1973 with Miller's support, Church remained in that position until his appointment as an international representative in 1975. Church rose quickly on the international staff, being promoted to deputy director of the contract department in 1976, to executive assistant to the UMW president later that same year, and finally to the Miller reelection ticket as candidate for UMW vice president in 1977.[83] Along the way, he developed a reputation as a loyal, strong-willed aide, who was not averse to settling an argument with his fists. A burly, forceful man, Sam Church was a tremendous contrast to the slight, indecisive Miller.[84]

8 The End of an Era: The 1979 Convention

ALTHOUGH Arnold Miller resigned his post as UMW president before the 1979 UMW convention, an account of the administrations led by Miller would be incomplete without a description of this meeting. In many ways, the 1979 convention wrote the bottom line on democracy under Miller's leadership. Despite his absence, Arnold Miller was probably as responsible for the process and substance of the Denver convention as the newly installed president, Sam Church.

Held in Denver, Colorado, from December 10 to December 20, the 1979 convention was the legacy of one of the most significant achievements of Miller's reform years—the resurrection of the UMW's constitutional convention as a mechanism for membership participation in, and control of, the administration of their union. The machinery necessary to accomplish this had been largely put in place during the 1973 and 1976 conventions. It remained intact for the 1979 convention. In addition, many of the delegates to the Denver meeting were veterans of the turbulent Pittsburgh and Cincinnati conventions. These delegates came to Denver more experienced in the democratic process and were thus better prepared to play a constructive, responsible role in the convention.

There were many differences between the Pittsburgh and

Cincinnati meetings and the Denver convention. In 1979, the new leadership of the UMW had a different approach to the convention as a democratic mechanism. This change was typified by Sam Church's firm style in the chair. The delegation, while better schooled in their role, came to Denver with a different attitude towards the constitutional convention as well. Undoubtedly affected by the events of recent years, the delegates appeared less enthusiastic about the convention as a democratic process and less aggressive within that process. As the pressures both on and within the union changed, so had the needs and the outlook of the union's members and officers. This was reflected in their actions and in their approach to the democratic convention process. In many ways, the Denver convention underscored both the achievements and the problems experienced by the UMW in the previous seven years.

As in 1976, delegates to the 1979 convention were elected according to the standards developed for the 1973 convention to ensure that the delegation was representative of the entire UMW membership and to prevent the stacking of the convention delegation to favor the leadership in power.[1] In Cincinnati, these standards had encouraged the increased participation of UMW members in the convention process. The same standards had different results in Denver three years later. Whereas 1,883 delegates represented an active UMW membership of 180,000 in 1976, only 1,267 delegates represented nearly 170,000 mine workers in 1979.[2] The active members-per-delegate ratio increased from 1 delegate per 95 members in Cincinnati to 134 members per delegate in Denver. This 33 percent drop in delegates combined with only a 6 percent decrease in active membership meant that a much lower percentage of the union's rank and file was participating in one of the union's most important democratic processes.

While it is very difficult to pin down the reasons for this phenomenon, one factor—cost—probably had a great influence. While the cost of transporting delegates to Colorado was picked up by the international, lost wages, hotel, and meal expenses were the responsibility of the local union.[3] Since each delegate could carry up to five votes, the local could save money by sending fewer delegates and assigning them more votes. The financial condition of many local unions after the 1977–78 contract strike probably forced many of them to reduce the number of delegates they sent to the convention. There is also some evidence of a change in attitude or loss of enthusiasm about the convention process between 1976 and 1979 that may have contributed to the fact that fewer miners were involved in the Denver meeting than in the previous convention.

Just as important to the convention process as the delegates, and in some respects even more important, are the convention committees. By analyzing and evaluating the resolutions submitted by the local unions, the committees, to a large degree, control what issues will appear before the convention and in what form. Until the constitution was changed during the 1976 convention, the UMW president had the right to appoint these committees. Seeing this as a powerful weapon that had, during the Lewis and Boyle years, been much abused, the Cincinnati convention voted to have the committees elected by votes at the district level. In 1979, for the first time in UMW history, each district convened a meeting of all its elected convention delegates before the convention and elected one of their number to serve on each of the nine convention committees.[4] This process was designed, in theory, to make the convention committees independent in their deliberations.

Whether or not these elected committees were any more independent than those chosen by Miller in 1973 and 1976 is difficult to determine. The committees appeared to function in almost perfect harmony with the union leadership. Most of the controversial proposals that Church supported were reported out with the committees' endorsement. The committees presented very few, if any, proposals that the leadership strongly opposed. While this convergence of opinion might have been coincidental, the UMW president, although stripped of the power to appoint the committees, still had input into the committee decision-making process. First, Church appointed each committee's chairperson from among the elected committee members, and he assigned staff members to advise and provide technical assistance to each committee. Second, from the first night when he was their host for dinner, through the several days before the convention when the committees met and transacted their business, Church and his aides were very visible in their active lobbying of the committees in session.[5] The insulated preconvention atmosphere, with only committees, staff, and officers present in Denver, offered a good opportunity for Church to impress his views on the committee members. All indications are that he was effective.

Technically, the work of most of the committees is based on resolutions submitted by local unions. This is another mechanism for involving the rank and file in the governance of their union and can therefore be viewed as a secondary measure of participation. In 1976, resolutions submitted filled 1,431 printed pages in the resolutions books. In 1979, the committees received only enough resolutions to fill 507 pages of the same size books, a 65 percent drop from the previous convention.[6]

Cost could not explain the decrease in resolutions as it could the decrease in the number of delegates. The attitude of rank-and-filers and officers at the local level probably had more to do with this decrease in participation. Events from 1976 to 1979 had a considerable effect on the outlook of the union's membership. The crisis of leadership, the health benefits and wildcat problems, the 110-day strike, and the seeming inability of the democratic system to deal with these problems had left considerable numbers of UMW members frustrated. When the time came to develop and draft convention resolutions, many miners quite probably felt that the whole process was pointless. Many UMW members undoubtedly believed that the near-chaos and anarchy that accompanied the 1976 convention made it improbable that much could be accomplished through such a forum. Certainly, many also remembered that very few of the collective bargaining demands endorsed by the Cincinnati convention were won at the bargaining table.

Whereas UMW members had looked to the 1976 convention with confidence and enthusiasm, as demonstrated by the large number of delegates and resolutions, skepticism and a lack of confidence in the democratic convention process probably better described the attitude in 1979. To many, the Cincinnati convention had been a debacle, and a repeat of the acrimony, dissent, and vigorous debate that brought that meeting to near-anarchy could bring the UMW to its knees. This fear of reliving the disorder of 1976, combined with several other factors, caused the disposition, and ultimately the performance, of the delegation to the Denver convention to differ markedly from the 1973 and 1976 delegations.

In 1976, the convention delegates had seemed determined to protect the democratic rights they had won. They appeared anxious to extend those rights even further. This was not the focus of the delegation in 1979. The majority of delegates came to Denver with a strong desire to bring unity to the UMW. Many of these delegates sought unity by assuming a passive, noncombative role during the proceedings and by accepting the lead of the chair. This acquiescence translated into the almost slavish acceptance of the chairman's rulings on votes, parliamentary questions, and procedural issues and into the delegates' endorsement of nearly all administration-backed proposals. Church, without prior experience in the chair of an international convention, skillfully took advantage of the delegation's cooperative attitude and was firmly in control throughout the Denver meeting. Ben Franklin, a *New York Times* reporter and long-time observer of the miners' union, summed up Church's mastery:

> By repeatedly invoking not only the memory of John L. Lewis but also some of his peremptory, gavel-banging, "the-ayes-have-it" style, he [Church] drove through most of a crucial agenda. . . . At the same time he was plainly winning the awe, if not the affection, of his peers.[7]

Church set the tone and established command of the proceedings on the first day of the convention. The initial matter to come before the convention was the partial report of the Credentials Committee. In the spirit of the 1976 convention, delegates immediately took to the floor to challenge the committee's recommendations, specifically their decision to grant credentials to delegates with fractional votes. Fractional votes occurred where locals sent more than one delegate for each vote they held. Thus some delegates carried only 0.50, 0.75, or some other fraction of a vote.[8] Since much of the convention's business was conducted by voice or standing votes, many felt these delegates would have a disproportionate influence on the voting. When a standing vote was taken on whether to accept the Credentials Committee report, which included the delegates with fractional votes, the delegation split almost fifty-fifty. The vote was so close that a roll call vote was called for. A roll call vote for a delegation of more than sixteen hundred usually takes several hours. Only one-half hour into the vote, after having polled only four of the twenty-one UMW districts, Church stepped to the mike:

"Now, Brothers, come to order a minute. Are we going to continue on with this or are we going to seat these delegates?"[9]

The delegation responded with an overwhelming vote to seat the delegates. At the press conference after the convention's first day, Church was asked if what he had done was constitutional. Church smiled and replied, "We did it, didn't we?"[10]

After this incident, the business of the convention went almost entirely Church's way. Several very important and controversial issues, which would probably have met with vehement opposition in 1976, were passed after minimal debate and with little opposition. The treatment of one such issue was representative of the proceedings and involved the method to be used to fill the vice president's position, left vacant when Sam Church was elevated to the union presidency upon Arnold Miller's resignation. Article V, Section 2, of the UMW constitution adopted at the 1976 convention stated, "If, at the time a vacancy occurs in the office of vice president, secretary-treasurer, or executive board member, more than two years of the term is unexpired, [the president] shall call for an election to fill the vacancy. . . ."[11] On the second day of the convention the Constitution Committee brought out a resolution proposing that this section of the constitution be amended to allow Church the one-time privilege of appointing his vice president, even though more than two years remained in the term.[12]

Even in the noncombative atmosphere of the Denver convention, the proposal to have an international officer of the UMW appointed by the president rather than elected by the membership stimulated one of the convention's liveliest debates. Numerous delegates vigorously opposed the resolution from the floor with remarks such as these:

Delegate James M. Branson, District 17, Charleston, W. Va.: I rise in opposition to the Majority report. What we've got here is not an issue of unity, it's an issue on democracy. Democracy strengthens the union. It doesn't weaken it. It doesn't disunite it. I think this resolution allowing appointment here is a waiving of the democratic process that we fought so hard for. I recognize the need to economize; but there's a whole lot of places that we can economize before we can start throwing democracy out the window.[13]

Delegate Clement Allen, District 5, Millsboro, Pa.: One winter Jock Yablonski, his wife and daughter were murdered because he stood up and fought for democracy. And I'm telling you right now, we have got to continue on. This is the labor reform union, the United Mine Workers of America. This is the only union that has total democracy and, by God, I'm telling you delegates right here and now, you better not yield it, because you know what you had before. . . . We cannot give up our democracy, and I will tell you right now I'm never going to give up my democracy.[14]

Other delegates rose to support the resolution, on grounds that an election would cost too much and would cause disunity at a time when the union was seeking financial and political stability:

Delegate Tomm D. Clark, District 12, Grayville, Illinois: I rise to support the majority opinion. It is the opinion of Local 1791, that we are proud . . . to be members of the most democratic union in the world. But we suggest to you . . . that an election at this time is a luxury we cannot afford. We suggest that we support Brother Sam in allowing him to appoint his vice president.[15]

The argument that appeared to turn the tide in favor of the proposal contended that this action was not a threat to democracy in the union, but rather a vote of confidence in Church and a vote for unifying the UMW behind him. This rationale was given credence in a speech from the floor by Lou Antal, president of District 5, early supporter of Jock Yablonski and Miners for Democracy, and one of the union's strongest advocates of democratic reform.

Delegate Lou Antal, District 5, Arnold, Pennsylvania: I
rise in support of the majority report. . . . As far as democracy and as far as fighting for it, I don't think there's
anybody here that fought harder than I did. I was with
Jock Yablonski. There were many here that were, and
they remember. And the idea wasn't that you're going to
take democracy away. You're not taking it away by the
appointing of a vice president on a temporary basis.
You're only putting your lead and trust in your leader
that you had affirmed yesterday.[16]

Shortly after Antal spoke, the convention voted decisively in a
voice vote to amend the constitution to allow Sam Church to
select a vice president.[17]

In the course of the ten-day meeting, the convention passed
several other controversial measures backed by the administration. Numerous delegates opposed at least some of these measures on the grounds that their passage would weaken the
democratic process and put more power into the hands of the
president and the IEB. The majority of delegates accepted
these measures quietly, "in the spirit of unity."

There appeared to be several reasons why the delegation
assumed the role it did. Most delegates wanted to avoid the
battles of earlier years and, instead, bring unity and solidarity
back to the union. Second, the political climate of the UMW
was much different than it was in 1976. In 1979, the leadership of the union would be firmly in control for at least two
more years; no election loomed just ahead as it had at Cincinnati. Thus candidates and their backers were not engaged in
jockeying for support and votes during the convention process. Third, the union and its members were still suffering the
financial and psychological effects of the 110-day strike of
1977–78. Their passive attitude was so different from 1976
that it almost appeared that the strike had taken the fight out
of many of the delegates. This, combined with the unstable
future of the coal industry, seemed responsible for the circle-
the-wagons, unity-at-all-costs mentality of many of the miners
in attendance. Fourth, much of the change can be attributed
to the change in leadership. Arnold Miller had some staunch
supporters and many bitter enemies, and thus had found it

difficult to unite a convention or the union behind him. While Church was not universally popular, he had not had time to develop very many strong opponents. Many of the delegates seemed to have an open mind toward their new president and wanted to give him a fair opportunity to get the union back on its feet.

Miller had run a very loose convention, emphasizing the need for an open meeting where as many delegates as possible could participate in the discussion and debate of the issues. He was not a dominant personality in the chair and did not lead the convention, but rather tried to keep it from getting out of control. Miller's conventions were both democratic and chaotic. Contrasted with the thin and wan Miller, Sam Church is a robust, powerful man who was an imposing figure in the chair and a strong, businesslike chairman who appeared as concerned with efficiency as he did with democracy. Delegates seemed almost intimidated by their new leader and rarely challenged his rulings or decisions on votes, some of which were extremely close. Church did not rule the convention with an iron fist, nor can it be said that he impeded the democratic process to the objection of the delegation. He did, however, sense the delegation's willingness, and maybe desire, to be guided by a firm hand.

The 1973 and 1976 UMW conventions had had tremendous influence on the mine workers' union, significantly altering its structure, administration, and policies. Although very different from these in nature and disposition, the 1979 convention also had important, if more subtle, effects on the union. The Denver convention came at a critical juncture in the UMW's history. The substantive measures passed at that meeting indicated that the union had chosen to follow a different course in the years ahead than it had followed in the recent past. Rather than the expansion and further development of democratic rights and processes that had occupied the time of the two previous conventions, the 1979 convention passed a number of measures that maintained, and in some cases, increased the power and control of the union's president. In addition to granting Church the authority to appoint his vice president on a one-time basis, the delegation approved constitutional amendments to affirm the president's power of appointment in some areas and expand it in other areas.

When the 1976 convention voted to have convention committees elected by votes at the district level, no provision was made for the selection of committee chairpersons or vice chairpersons. The practice of having the president appoint chairpersons thus remained in practice in 1979. On the convention's second day the Constitution Committee proposed an amendment to legitimize this practice by constitutionally empowering the president to appoint, from among the delegates elected to each committee, the respective committee chairpersons. This power of appointment is significant because each committee chairperson could, potentially, exercise great influence on the work of that committee. The Constitution Committee motion also proposed, as a compromise, that the committee vice chairpersons be elected by each respective committee. After a very close voice vote, the amendment was approved by a standing vote, 671 in favor, 556 opposed.[18]

A third controversial motion concerning the issue of appointment versus election centered on the jobs of organizers, safety coordinators and inspectors, and Coal Miners' Political Action Committee (COMPAC) representatives. Historically, as in most unions, the president of the union had the constitutional authority to make these appointments. The 1976 convention, in one of its most heated debates, had considered the possibility of electing these officials on a district basis, and in a very close and controversial vote, the delegation agreed to continue the practice of having the president fill the positions by appointment.[19] Although more than one hundred resolutions supporting the election of organizers, safety staffers, and COMPAC representatives were submitted to the 1979 convention, the Constitution Committee in Denver recommended that the positions remain appointive. A minority report of the committee opposing the continuation of presidential appointment to these jobs, was presented, and a number of delegates spoke from the floor in support of the minority report's position. The pitch of the debate in 1979, however, was far less fervent than at the previous convention, the proponents of elections far less zealous. When the voice vote was taken, the delegation approved the majority report, thus preserving the president's right of appointment.[20]

The fourth issue concerning appointments involved a proposal to expand the president's power to include the appointment of interim IEB members. Before 1979, the UMWA constitution provided that an election be held for an IEB seat that became vacant with more than two years of the term unexpired. At Denver, the constitution committee proposed a new section to the constitution, Article V, Section 22, giving the president the authority to appoint an interim board member until the required election could be held. With the constitution requiring only that the vote "be held as promptly as possible," this proposal gave the president the opportunity to handpick a candidate for the IEB who might serve for a considerable period of time before an election was scheduled. This also enabled the president to bestow an incumbency upon his favorite candidate. The committee's proposal limited this virtually open-ended appointment to vacancies occurring due to illness, death, or resignation, requiring that a vacancy occurring due to suspension be filled by election in ninety days. Since the constitution already granted the president the power to fill by appointment any vacant IEB seat with less than two years remaining in the term, this proposal expanded the president's power of appointment regarding the IEB to cover most contingencies. This expansion did not seem to concern the delegates at Denver. When Article V, Section 22, came to the floor it met no debate and was passed by acclamation.[21]

On most other important issues dealt with by the 1979 convention, some of which were highly controversial, the delegates approved administration-backed proposals. Perhaps the most difficult, and potentially most explosive, proposal concerned a dues increase. In 1973, the Pittsburgh convention voted to raise monthly dues for UMW members from $5.50 to $12.00. There was no change in the dues amount at the 1976 Cincinnati convention. On the third day of the 1979 convention in Denver, the Constitution Committee, with the full support of Church, recommended a constitutional amendment that would more than double the $12.00 monthly dues requirement. The committee's proposal would change the dues structure from a flat dollar amount to a formula of three hours wages, at the lowest underground miners' wage rate, per month. This formula would have set dues at $26.69 a month, a 122 percent increase. The committee urged that the dues increase was necessary because of inflation, legal judgments, and the need to increase organizing efforts. The hourly formula was recommended by the committee because it would tie future dues increases to the union's gains at the bargaining table.[22]

The UMW leadership undoubtedly expected a tough fight would be required to win such a large increase. With inflation rampant, dissatisfaction with the international widespread, and miners still reeling financially from the last strike, this did not seem like an auspicious occasion to ask for such a large dues increase. These factors apparently did not trouble the delegates. Although this issue prompted one of the longest debates of the convention, the speakers were heavily in favor of granting the proposed dues hike.[23]

Most of the supporters of the dues motion pointed to the need for a financially strong and stable organization. Many also saw the issue, once again, as a vote of confidence in their new president. Delegate John R. Bowyer of Cumberland, Kentucky, summed up the sentiments of most of the speakers favoring an increase when he spoke from the floor:

> Brother Sam Church said when we left this convention that he was going to let the coal operators in America know that the United Mine Workers were here still strong and surviving. So let's give him the leadership and let's give him the money to do this. Let's go forth from here and have a union that will be heard throughout America. Let's let them know we're strong and we're willing to dig in our pockets for a little bit of money.[24]

Of the thirty-six delegates who spoke on the dues issue only twelve opposed the proposed increase. Despite the seemingly strong support for the motion, voice and standing ballots failed to resolve the issue, and a roll call vote was called for. The motion carried by a vote of 1,181 for the dues hike and 912 against, a margin of only 269.[25]

A second financial question brought before the convention involved the initiation fee required of new UMW members.

The 1973 convention raised the initiation fee for membership in the UMW from fifty dollars to one hundred dollars. At Denver, the Constitution Committee supported a resolution calling for a doubling of the initiation fee to two hundred dollars. Backed by Church, the motion met little resistance and was passed by a voice vote.[26]

A third Church administration victory on financial issues came on the question of a selective strike assessment. This issue arose as a result of one of the major coal producers' withdrawal from the BCOA. Consolidation Coal (Consol) left the operator's group in May 1979, ostensibly because of its unhappiness with the BCOA's role as the industry's bargaining representative the previous year.[27] As an independent coal company, Consol would not be obligated to accept a BCOA-UMW agreement. The selective strike concept was one way of pressuring Consol to accept the terms of a BCOA-UMW contract. By creating a strike fund through the assessment of miners working under a signed BCOA-UMW agreement, the UMW could strike Consol's operations while paying Consol strikers 65 percent or more of their regular pay, enabling the UMW to endure a long strike against Consol with minimal losses. This whipsaw tactic could be an extremely effective strategy. Its success depended on getting the convention delegation in Denver to empower the international union, through the IEB, to require yet another financial contribution to the union. The passage of such an assessment was further complicated by tradition since the UMW had never, since the 1920s, had a strike fund or strike assessment.[28]

When the Constitution Committee's recommendation to incorporate the selective strike assessment into the union's constitution hit the floor it met the same compliant reception as most of the other administration-backed proposals. Debate was short, with one delegate's remarks being representative of the majority of the delegation:

> Delegate Ernest Moore, District 29, Thorpe, West Virginia: We have a new president and I am satisfied. If he says "Work", we are going to work. If he says "Strike", we are going to strike. But the only thing this section is saying to the coal operators who are pulling out from the BCOA,

"If you are divided, we are not going to let you divide us."[29]

Passed on a voice vote, the acceptance of this amendment indicated that the delegates' confidence in the new president extended to his role as chief bargainer for the union.[30]

All Church's victories were not so easy. On one important financial question the administration nearly suffered a loss. On the convention's fourth day, the Constitution Committee proposed an administration-backed change in Article XIII, Section 6, of the constitution that would have given the IEB the unlimited right to assess the membership in order to pay the costs of legal actions and judgments against the union. Coming on the heels of the 122 percent dues increase, the delegation expressed overwhelming opposition to the motion. On a voice vote, the proposal was voted down decisively, thus sending it back to the committee.[31] When the resolution was brought back on the convention's sixth day, the only change in the provision's language was the inclusion of a twenty-dollar-per-year cap on the assessment. After some of the convention's liveliest debate, a voice vote approved the revised amendment.[32] Church, however, received a setback on the seventh day of the meeting when the delegates called for a roll call vote to reconsider the action on the twenty-dollar assessment. After a successful vote to reconsider, the delegates approved a similar assessment providing for a maximum levy of ten dollars per year.[33] Although Church cheerfully volunteered that "you can't win 'em all," after the vote, it probably would not be accurate to term this turn of events a defeat for the administration.[34] The international had gained one more way of raising funds, and despite the delegation's reneging on the twenty-dollar assessment, it did meet the leadership halfway on this issue.

Although much more time was spent on the report of the Constitution Committee than on any other report, other committees did present reports on which the delegates took action. The Collective Bargaining Committee's report generated interest among the delegates, although this enthusiasm was tempered by the knowledge that in 1977–78 the negotiating team had been unable to win more than a few of the demands endorsed at the Cincinnati convention. The report, and the delegates' action on it, did provide some insight into the bargaining priorities of the UMW membership. Among the list of demands endorsed by the delegation were "a substantial wage increase," an unlimited cost-of-living adjustment, supplemental unemployment benefits (SUB) to help during layoffs, longer vacations, extended sick leave, and more holidays. The delegates also called for revisions in the contractual dispute settlement mechanism, including the abolition of the Arbitration Review Board. Conspicuous by its absence was any reference to the right-to-strike principle that had been a major bone of contention in the 1977–78 negotiations.[35]

Most of the other committee reports were accepted in whole or largely intact. Consistent with the acquiescent nature of the 1979 convention, the recommendations of the Health and Safety, Health and Retirement, Organizing, COMPAC/Legislative, and Resolutions Committees met with little discussion and even less dissent.[36]

In sum, the 1979 convention witnessed some fundamental changes in substance and attitude on the part of both the union's leadership and the rank and file. Rather than seizing the convention as an opportunity to direct and influence the organization and its leadership, the delegates, representing the UMW membership, abdicated their leadership role to the newly installed president, Sam Church, and passively followed the lead of their president by endorsing nearly all administration-backed proposals. As a result, the union's international officers emerged with increased power and control in several important areas.

The action taken by the convention probably does not, in any major way, undermine the democratic gains won by the union over the previous seven years. Structurally, district autonomy, free and fair elections, open conventions, and a more open bargaining process, including membership input and contract ratification, remained in place. The Denver convention, however, did point up a marked decline in enthusiasm, at least among the delegates, for an active, open, rank-and-file convention in which the membership of the union tells its elected leaders what to do rather than rubber-stamps the preconceived policies of the leadership. While this kind of acquiescence and compliance might have been the best policy to bring unity and stability to the mine workers' union and while the UMW membership might have found a strong and capable leader who would not emasculate the democratic gains the rank and file had won, the proceedings at Denver had as much in common with the less than democratic charades that passed for conventions under Lewis and Boyle as they did with the 1973 and 1976 Miller conventions. Perhaps the UMW membership skillfully and consciously sought a happy medium between the autocracy and stability of the union under Lewis and Boyle and the democracy and instability of the union under Miller. Or perhaps the UMW membership had lost patience and become frustrated with the chaos and disorder that inevitably must accompany the transition from a very undemocratic union to a very democratic one, choosing the devil they knew over the devil they were still getting to know.

The membership of the UMW, through their delegates to the 1979 convention, left the answer to where the union is going largely in the hands of their new president, Sam Church. But they also left in place the democratic mechanisms through which to regain control of their union, should their leadership fail or falter.

9 The Reform Movement in Perspective

VOTED into office as the standard bearers of the Miners for Democracy reform movement, Arnold Miller, Mike Trbovich, and Harry Patrick carried a mandate from the membership of the union to remake the UMW into an open, responsive, and democratic labor organization. The opportunity and challenge was virtually unprecedented on the modern American labor scene. The experience of the UMW during the reform administration's first five-year term and during the two years of Miller's unfinished second term has important ramifications not only for coal miners, but for union members and their organizations throughout the labor movement.

Without question, the efforts of Miller's first administration to bring about significant changes in the structure and administration of the UMW were successful. In its earliest days, the reform leadership took action to purge the union of the neglectful, nepotistic, and often corrupt atmosphere in which the past administration conducted union affairs by removing Tony Boyle's appointees and scheduling elections for all district offices. The convention mechanism was resurrected and reconstructed in order to involve the rank and file more directly in the decision-making process.

Under Miller's leadership, the union convention became the

chief vehicle for pursuing democratic reform within the mine workers' union. The 1973 and 1976 conventions made whole-sale changes in union structure and policies that laid the foundations for democratic unionism. Delegates to these conventions approved provisions to ensure full district autonomy and honest elections at all levels of the union, fair procedures for intraunion trials of officers and members, measures to make officers and IEB members more accountable to the membership, and guidelines that delineated more exactly the power and responsibilities of these elected union officials. The conventions also made changes in the convention process that attempted to make the convention itself truly democratic.

The Pittsburgh and Cincinnati conventions approved major reforms in another area, the collective bargaining process. The restructured collective bargaining procedure allowed greater rank-and-file involvement in this most important area by including the membership in every step of the process—from the formulation of initial demands to the decision to accept a contract. Putting this newfound democracy into practice for the 1974 industrywide negotiations, the UMW emerged with a bench mark contract that made significant advances in a number of crucial areas.

In the later part of Miller's first term and during the two years of his second term, however, the movement toward democratic reform ground to a halt. Many observers of the reform process feel that the pendulum swung back during the period of the 1977–78 contract strike and the 1979 convention and that the union became less democratic and more autocratic. Former UMW secretary-treasurer Harry Patrick contends that the union has come full circle and is really no further ahead than it was under Boyle: "All of the things we fought for in 1972, . . ." says Patrick "it's all right back where we started."[1] The 1979 convention, the return of Cadillac limousines, the increase in salaries and expenses, and the general trend, in both action and attitude, toward the centralization of power and authority in the union's leadership is convincing evidence to support Patrick's belief.

A closer examination of the UMW's experience during the Miller years, however, reveals that the union is not back where it

155

started. While the reform movement may be dead or dying and progress toward further democratic reform may be halted, the union was made an unquestionably more progressive, open, and responsive organization than it was under Tony Boyle. And despite the fact that some of the substantive reforms and some of the democratic spirit may have been lost during the later years of Miller's time in office, most of the democratic laws, practices, procedures, and policies created during the reform period are alive. Most have been institutionalized and can be changed only by a vote of the union convention. It is unlikely the membership will surrender these rights they fought so hard for or be seduced into giving them up as happened in the past, since, more than anything else, the membership has developed a democratic consciousness that will not die easily.

It seems clear that the reform movement's effect on the mine workers' union was substantial. It is much less clear whether the democratic reform movement in the UMW had the influence on the labor movement generally that many had hoped and predicted it would. The 1970s witnessed the rise of reform-minded challenges to the established leadership of some of the key labor organizations in this country. This phenomenon was probably not purely coincidental. The rise of the dissident group Steelworkers Fight Back, as the base of support for Ed Sadlowski's run for the presidency of the United Steelworkers of America in 1976 against the establishment candidate, Lloyd McBride, is the most significant example of this trend. The emergence of Teamsters for a Democratic Union (TDU) and the Professional Drivers Council (PROD) as reform-minded opposition groups within the powerful Teamsters organization are other important examples. It is difficult, however, to establish the extent to which the mine workers' experience influenced these reform efforts.

Undoubtedly, MFD's success served as an inspiration to these reform groups, and some of the activists who were intimately involved in MFD's successful challenge advised, supported, and, in some cases, even worked directly in these other reform movements. Edgar James, a close aide to Arnold Miller before and after his election, later managed Sadlowski's campaign for a time. Another individual who played a significant role in MFD's victory and who was also involved in the Sadlowski challenge was liberal activist and lawyer Joseph Rauh.[2] Apparently there never was, however, any formal tie between the Miller administration and Sadlowski's organization. Also, there were important differences between MFD, Sadlowski's effort, and the other dissident groups in origin, aims, strategies, and the circumstances surrounding their challenges. Of course, the effects each group had on the union hierarchy it challenged were vastly different. Contrasted with MFD's election victory, Sadlowski ran a strong but unsuccessful race against McBride. His influence beyond the campaign was minimal. TDU and PROD are still alive and actively sniping at the well-entrenched Teamster leadership. Their significance, to date, has been so minor that they have been largely ignored by the membership they sought to rouse.

The threat that MFD and these other reform movements posed may have brought about some constructive movement on the part of the hierarchies in the Steelworkers, Teamsters, and in other unions. It has not, however, altered in any identifiable fashion the way unions are governed in this country. If MFD has had an influence beyond the mine workers' union, it has been a subtle and not a substantial one.

The mine workers' union faces challenges on many fronts that will influence what direction the UMW will take in the years ahead. The economics of the coal industry is one factor that will have a significant impact on the union. The progress and militance of any labor organization in terms of dealing with employers is directly related to the economic environment it must exist in. Between 1972 and 1977, the years of Miller's first term, the coal industry was booming. There was a shortage of miners, jobs were secure, and demand was high. Companies were concerned with maintaining increasing production, a situation that gave the UMW considerable leverage at all levels. Since 1977 the demand for production has eased. The steel industry, a large buyer of coal, has fallen on hard times, and increasingly stringent pollution controls have severely cut back the demand for the high-sulfur coal mined in Ohio and northern West Virginia. This has resulted in mine shutdowns and layoffs. By late summer 1980, at least twenty-two thousand miners throughout the United States had been laid off.[3]

The weak state of the coal industry, along with the hardnosed stance the operators have taken on wildcats and in the 1977–78 contract talks, have combined to soften the militance of both the leadership and the membership. One indication of this change is the fact that since the settlement of March 1978, wildcat strikes in the coalfields are down almost 90 percent to a ten-year low.[4] What effect this change in attitude will have on internal union affairs and whether this attitude will significantly influence industry bargaining scheduled for early 1981 remain to be seen.

A second challenge that the UMW faces is posed by management, not by the small-time coal companies that the union once fought but by multinational energy conglomerates such as EXXON, Gulf, and Conoco. These corporations are devouring existing coal companies and potential coal reserves with an increasing appetite. In the West they pose the greatest threat. There, coal seams are much larger and richer and are more easily mined than in Appalachia, thus creating a dramatic difference in production per man. These factors, combined with the conglomerates' desire to keep the UMW out, are responsible for many western miners making more than a hundred dollars a day, wages considerably higher than the average UMW member.[5] The high wage scale, the lack of a union heritage on the part of many western miners, and the infighting and instability of the union leadership in the past several years have made UMW organizing drives unsuccessful. Failure to organize western coal is significant since coal reserves in the West are much greater than in the eastern coalfields. With coal production shifting to the West, the UMW's share of national coal production has shrunk from more than 70 percent in 1970 to less than 50 percent.[6] In order to deal with this problem, the 1979 UMW convention voted to significantly expand the union's organizing efforts both in the East and in the West. Sam Church has pledged a major share of a large dues increase to expand the number of organizers and support staff.[7] If the union's efforts to organize the large nonunion sector of the industry are not successful, this will seriously weaken the union's power base in the future.

The UMW and democratic reform are at a critical point. But

all prospects are not dim for the miners' union. Externally, chances are good that market conditions will improve. The weak economic state of the coal industry appears to be only temporary. The oil shortage and continual price increases, combined with advances in coal conversion technology and increased distrust of nuclear energy, give coal a bright future. This would almost certainly strengthen the UMW's bargaining position and restore the militance of its membership in the years ahead.[8]

Internally, some semblance of unity has returned to the mine workers' union. At least for the moment, Sam Church has gained the confidence and respect of much of the UMW membership. Although his background and his performance in the chair at the Denver convention have left many wondering about his commitment to union democracy, Church, at this point, cannot be accused of being undemocratic or unresponsive. If the union leadership shows respect for the membership and for the democratic processes that have been put into place over the last seven years and if UMW members jealously guard the democratic rights they have won, the miners' union could remain a strong and democratic labor organization.

When he took office in 1972, Arnold Miller made a pledge to a group of coal miners:

> Every coal miner will know this is his union. It no longer belongs to one man. . . We're going to go out and resolve the problems we have and make this union the greatest union in the country, as it once was.[9]

The achievements of the Miller years have been great, and today, despite the stagnation of reform, the UMW belongs to the membership to a greater extent than anytime in the last fifty years. Yet the problems encountered over the seven years that Arnold Miller headed the union have also been great. Much progress has been made, but miners are used to hard fights and bad odds. The future of the coal industry is bright and so, potentially, is the future of the United Mine Workers of America.

Notes

Introduction

1. Jack Barbash, "Union Democracy," *Daily Labor Report*, November 25, 1957, p. E-2.

Chapter 1

1. McAlister Coleman, *Men and Coal* (New York: Farrar and Rinehart, 1943), p. 53.

2. "International Officers Honored by Reelection," *United Mine Workers Journal* (hereafter cited as *UMW Journal*), February 15, 1921, p. 5.

3. Melvyn Dubofsky and Warren Van Tine, *John L. Lewis: A Biography* (New York: Quadrangle, 1977), pp. 112–13.

4. Ibid., pp. 115–22.

5. Paul John Nyden, "Miners for Democracy: Struggle in the Coal Fields" (Ph.D. dissertation, Columbia University, 1974), pp. 413–17, 466–67.

6. Dubofsky and Van Tine, *John L. Lewis*, pp. 125–27.

7. John Brophy, *A Miner's Life* (Madison: University of Wisconsin Press, 1964), p. 214.

8. Dubofsky and Van Tine, *John L. Lewis*, pp. 127–28.

9. Brophy, *A Miner's Life*, pp. 217–18.

10. Ibid., p. 218.

11. Ibid., p. 230.

12. United Mine Workers of America, UMWA Constitution, 1920, Article III, Section 3. In all subsequent notes referring to official union documents, the United Mine Workers of America is cited as UMW.

13. Coleman, *Men and Coal*, pp. 126–27.

14. UMW, *Proceedings of the Thirtieth Consecutive Constitutional Convention, Indianapolis, Indiana, January 25–February 2, 1927.*

15. Ibid., p. 452.

16. Dubofsky and Van Tine, *John L. Lewis*, pp. 159–60, 162–65.

17. Ibid. and Reorganized United Mine Workers of America, *Proceedings of the National Convention of the United Mine Workers of America, Reorganized, Springfield, Illinois, March 10 to March 15, 1930*, pp. 11–23.

18. UMW, *Proceedings of the Thirty-first Consecutive Constitutional Convention, Indianapolis, Indiana, March 10 to March 20, 1930*, pp. 484–85.

19. Ibid.

20. Dubofsky and Van Tine, *John L. Lewis*, pp. 118–19, 157–58.

21. UMW, *Proceedings of the Thirty-fourth Constitutional Convention of the United Mine Workers of America, Washington, D.C., January 28 to February 7, 1936;* the roll call vote in 1936 was over the issue of district autonomy. The next roll call vote at a UMW convention did not take place until 1973 when the convention voted on a dues increase. UMW, *Proceedings of the Forty-sixth Consecutive Constitutional Convention of the United Mine Workers of America, Pittsburgh, Pennsylvania, December 3 to December 14, 1973*, pp. 264–65.

22. Dubofsky and Van Tine, *John L. Lewis*, pp. 169–70.

23. Ibid., pp. 171–72, and Nyden, "Miners For Democracy," pp. 440–68.

24. Alden Whitman, "John L. Lewis: A Fighting Leader," *New York Times*, June 12, 1969, p. 34.

25. UMW, *John L. Lewis and the International Union, United Mine Workers of America* (Washington, D.C.: UMWA, 1952), p. 250.

26. Dubofsky and Van Tine, *John L. Lewis*, p. 190.

27. Richard A. Lester, *As Unions Mature* (Princeton, N.J.: Princeton University Press, 1966), p. 100.

28. Dubofsky and Van Tine, *John L. Lewis*, pp. 374–75, 378–81.

29. Ibid., pp. 389–94, 397–404, 415–40.

30. In 1978 the names of these funds were changed to UMWA Health and Retirement Funds.

31. Joseph E. Finley, *The Corrupt Kingdom: The Rise and Fall of the United Mine Workers* (New York: Simon & Schuster, 1972), pp. 178–204.

32. Keith Dix et al., *Work Stoppages and the Grievance Procedure in the Appalachian Coal Industry* (Morgantown: West Virginia University Institute for Labor Studies, 1972), p. 7.

33. Nyden, "Miners for Democracy," p. 305.

34. UMW, *Proceedings of the Thirty-fifth Constitutional Convention, Washington, D.C., January 25 to February 3, 1938*, p. 434.

35. Ibid., p. 438.

36. UMW, *Proceedings of the Fortieth Consecutive Convention, Cincinnati, Ohio, October 5 to October 12, 1948*, p. 441.

37. Saul Alinsky, *John L. Lewis: An Unauthorized Biography* (New York: G. P. Putnam's Sons, 1970), p. 350.

38. Ibid.

39. Finley, *Corrupt Kingdom*, p. 170–71.

40. Ibid., p. 171.

41. Ibid.

42. "John L. Lewis Goes to Bat Again," *Business Week*, October 4, 1958, p. 97.

43. Finley, *Corrupt Kingdom*, pp. 172, 188–97.

44. Ibid., pp. 163–68.

45. Brit Hume, *Death and the Mines: Rebellion and Murder in the United Mine Workers* (New York: Grossman Publishers, 1971), p. 23, and Finley, *Corrupt Kingdom*, pp. 174–75.

46. Finley, *Corrupt Kingdom*, pp. 174–75, 199–202.

47. "Lewis Goes to Bat Again," p. 97.

48. "Miners Seek a Pact in Cool, Quiet Talks," *Business Week*, September 28, 1968, p. 109.

49. Dubofsky and Van Tine, *John L. Lewis*, p. 504.

50. UMW, *It's Your Union. Pass It On.: Officers' Report to the 47th Constitutional Convention, Cincinnati, Ohio, September, 1976*, p. 27.

51. Nyden, "Miners for Democracy," pp. 476, 484–89.

52. Finley, *Corrupt Kingdom,* p. 241.

53. Ibid., pp. 241–42.

54. Ibid., p. 242.

55. UMW, *Proceedings of the Forty-fourth Consecutive Constitutional Convention of the United Mine Workers of America, Bal Harbour, Florida, September 1 to 11, 1964.*

56. Hume, *Death and the Mines,* pp. 43–52, and Finley, *Corrupt Kingdom,* p. 243.

57. Hume, *Death and the Mines,* pp. 62–66, 69–71.

58. "Miners Seek a Pact," p. 109, and Nyden, "Miners for Democracy," pp. 475, 483.

59. Nyden, "Miners for Democracy," pp. 475, 483.

60. Hume, *Death and the Mines,* p. 16.

61. Ibid., pp. 94–152, and Nyden, "Miners for Democracy," p. 477.

62. Hume, *Death and the Mines,* pp. 170–71.

63. Ibid., p. 173.

64. Suzanne Crowell, "Leadership Contest Shakes up UMWA," *Southern Patriot,* October 1969, p. 1.

65. Jeanne Rasmussen, "The Miner: What Happens Now," *Mountain Life and Work,* February 1970.

66. Nyden, "Miners for Democracy," pp. 492–502.

67. Ibid., p. 514.

68. "Official UMWA Election Returns," *UMW Journal,* January 15, 1970, p. 3.

69. "A Message to the Members of the UMWA," *UMW Journal,* May 15, 1972, p. 2.

70. Nyden, "Miners for Democracy," pp. 518–26.

71. Ibid.

72. Ben A. Franklin, "Reform Miners Select Candidates to Run against Boyle," *New York Times,* May 29, 1972, p. 14.

73. Ben A. Franklin, "Angry U.M.W. Insurgent, Arnold Ray Miller," *New York Times,* May 30, 1972, p. 14.

74. Ibid.

75. Franklin, "Reform Miners Select Candidates," p. 14.

76. Nyden, "Miners for Democracy," pp. 532–40.

77. Miners for Democracy, *The Miner's Voice*, June 1972, pp. 5–6.

78. Ibid., p. 7.

79. Nyden, "Miners for Democracy," p. 583.

80. Ibid., pp. 562–63.

81. Ben A. Franklin, "Mine Union Found Liable in Civil Suit over Funds," *New York Times*, April 29, 1971, p. 1.

82. "Mine Workers: Their Chief Is Convicted," *New York Times*, April 2, 1972, sec. 4, p. 2.

83. Finley, *Corrupt Kingdom*, pp. 36–39.

84. "Miller, Trbovich, Patrick Win Top UMWA Positions," *UMW Journal*, December 1973, p. 3.

85. Thomas Bethell, "A Mine Disaster; A Last Ditch Resistance; A Happy Inaugural; and Tough Times to Come," *Coal Patrol* 31 (January 1, 1973), p. 7.

86. "The Martyr Had Been Vindicated," *New York Times*, December 17, 1973, p. E2.

Chapter 2

1. "Miller Orders Full District Elections," *UMW Journal*, December 1972, p. 4.

2. Ibid.

3. "New Officers, Staff Cut Salaries," *UMW Journal*, February 1, 1973, p. 3.

4. "First Nine District Elections Set," *UMW Journal*, February 15, 1973, p. 8.

5. Ben A. Franklin, "Miners Now Have Problems of Free Choice," *New York Times*, November 30, 1975, sec. 4, p. 4.

6. "Reform Movement of MFD Gone, But Spirit Remains," *Fairmont* (W. Va.) *Times-West Virginian*, June 5, 1977, p. 8-A.

7. Ibid.

8. John P. Moody, "New District 5 Chief Louis Antal Urges Rejuvenation of UMW," *Pittsburgh Post-Gazette*, July 2, 1973, p. 3.

9. "Winners Want MFD Put to Rest," *Charleston* (W. Va.) *Gazette,* June 1, 1973, p. 16-A.

10. James Craft, "Transition in the Mine Workers Union and the Impact on Labor Relations," *Pittsburgh Business Review,* Summer 1976, p. 2.

11. For 1972 international election results, see "Miller, Trbovich, Patrick Win Top UMWA Positions," *UMW Journal,* December 1972, pp. 3–4. For results of district elections, see "Seven More District Elections Held," *UMW Journal,* June 1–15, 1973, p. 3; "Reform Slate Wins District 2 Elections," *UMW Journal,* June 1–15, 1973, p. 12; "More District Elections," *UMW Journal,* September 1973, p. 15; "District Conventions, Elections Continue," *UMW Journal,* October 1–15, 1973, p. 14; "Elections in 19, 28, 29," *UMW Journal,* November 1–15, 1973, p. 7; "District 28 Results," *UMW Journal,* November 16–30, 1973, p. 3. For a capsule account of the district elections, see Paul John Nyden, "Miners for Democracy: Struggle in the Coalfields" (Ph.D. dissertation, Columbia University, 1974), pp. 833–45.

12. UMW, *The Year of the Rank and File, 1973: Officers' Report to the United Mine Workers of America Forty-sixth Constitutional Convention, Pittsburgh, Pennsylvania,* December 1973, pp. 74–81.

13. See, for example, "If You Work at a Mine Listed Below—Watch Out," *UMW Journal,* July 15–31, 1973, pp. 12–13, and "Supreme Court Hears Key Safety Cases," *UMW Journal,* October 16–31, 1973, p. 8.

14. Joseph E. Finley, *The Corrupt Kingdom: The Rise and Fall of the United Mine Workers* (New York: Simon & Schuster, 1972), pp. 200–202.

15. UMW, *Year of the Rank and File,* pp. 120–23, and "Fund Report," *UMW Journal,* October 1–15, 1973, pp. 4–13.

16. UMW, *Year of the Rank and File,* p. 102.

17. Ibid., pp. 107–11.

18. Ibid., p. 136, and "Coal Miners' Money Working for Coal Miners," *UMW Journal,* July 15–31, 1973, p. 24.

19. "UMW Convention Set for Pittsburgh in December," *UMW Journal,* May 15–31, 1973, p. 9.

20. UMW, *Proceedings of the Forty-sixth Consecutive Constitutional Convention of the United Mine Workers of America, Pittsburgh, Pennsylvania, December 3–14, 1973,* introduction.

21. Ibid.

22. Ibid. Other premises involved using the convention as an "educational experience" for delegates and identifying new leadership from the rank and file.

23. "Dues Not Required for UMWA Pension; Bogey Locals Must Merge with Active Locals," *UMW Journal*, February 1, 1973, p. 3.

24. UMW, *Proceedings of the Convention, 1973*, introduction.

25. Ibid.

26. Ibid.

27. Ibid.

28. Ibid., p. 25.

29. Ibid., introduction.

30. Ibid., p. 29.

31. Ibid., p. 19.

32. Ibid., introduction.

33. Ibid., p. 31.

34. Ibid., p. 386.

35. Ibid., p. 266.

36. Matt Witt, "New Constitution Guarantees Members' Right to Democracy," *UMW Journal*, January 1–15, 1974, p. 11.

37. Ibid.

38. UMW, UMWA Constitution, 1973, Article VI, Section 3.

39. Ibid., Section 16.

40. Ibid., Section 17.

41. Witt, "New Constitution Guarantees Members' Right to Democracy," p. 14.

42. Ibid., p. 12.

43. Ibid.

44. Ibid., pp. 13–14.

45. Ibid., p. 14.

46. UMW, *Proceedings of the Convention, 1973*, p. 439.

Chapter 3

1. UMW, UMWA Constitution, 1971.

2. Don Stillman, "The UMWA Convention: Democracy in Action," *UMW Journal,* January 1–15, 1974, pp. 4–6.

3. UMW, *Proceedings of the Forty-sixth Consecutive Constitutional Convention of the United Mine Workers of America, Pittsburgh, Pennsylvania, December 3–14, 1973,* pp. 80–82; also UMWA Constitution, 1973, Article XIX, Sections 1–5, and 7.

4. UMW, *Proceedings of the Convention, 1973,* p. 80.

5. Ibid.

6. Ibid.

7. Ibid., p. 81.

8. Ibid.

9. Ibid., p. 82.

10. Ibid.

11. "How Collective Bargaining Works" and "Bargaining Structure," *UMW Journal,* April 16–30, 1974, pp. 6–7.

12. UMW, *Proceedings of the Convention, 1973,* p. 46.

13. Ibid., pp. 477–527.

14. Stillman, "The UMWA Convention," pp. 8–10.

15. See *UMW Journal,* and in particular, "The 1974 Contract," April 16–30, 1974, pp. 5–11; "First District Bargaining Conference Held," May 16–31, 1974, pp. 4–7; "Negotiators Debate UMWA Demands" and "UMWA 1974 Contract Demands," September 16–30, 1974, pp. 4–25; and "The Proposed Contract," November 1974, pp. 1–48.

16. Data include all *UMW Journals* during years 1964, 1968, 1971, and 1974.

17. Tom Bethell, "It's Our Time to Catch Up," *UMW Journal,* October 16–31, 1974, p. 10.

18. "First District Bargaining Conference Held," *UMW Journal,* May 16–31, 1974, pp. 4–5.

19. Ibid.

20. Ibid., p. 5.

21. Don Stillman, "UMWA Presents Contract Demands," *UMW Journal,* September 1–15, 1974, p. 3.

22. Ibid.

23. Don Stillman, "BCOA Rejects Most UMWA Proposals," *UMW Journal*, October 1–15, 1974, p. 7.

24. Don Stillman, "Operators Move to Force Coal Strike," *UMW Journal*, October 16–31, 1974, p. 3.

25. UMW, *It's Your Union. Pass It On.: Officers' Report to the Forty-seventh Constitutional Convention, Cincinnati, Ohio, September 1976*, p. 21.

26. Ben A. Franklin, "Coal Union Seeks New Concessions," *New York Times*, November 27, 1974, p. 1.

27. UMW, *Officers' Report, 1976*, p. 22.

28. Ben A. Franklin, "Mine Union Panel Backs Coal Pact," *New York Times*, November 27, 1974, p. 1.

29. "How Rank and File Ratification Works," *UMW Journal*, November 1974, pp. 10–11.

30. UMW, *Officers' Report, 1976*, p. 22.

31. Ibid., pp. 22–23.

32. Ibid., p. 23.

33. "Rank-and-File Approves Contract," *UMW Journal*, December 1974, p. 3.

34. Ibid.

35. UMW, *Officers' Report, 1976*, p. 23.

36. "Major Economic Contract Gains," *UMW Journal*, November 1974, p. 4.

37. UMW, *Officers' Report, 1976*, p. 27.

38. Stillman, "BCOA Rejects Most UMWA Proposals," p. 7.

39. As quoted in UMW, *Officers' Report, 1976*, p. 15.

Chapter 4

1. D. Byron Yake, "Trbovich Breaks Silence on Feud," *Charleston* (W. Va.) *Gazette*, November 8, 1975, p. 1-A.

2. UMW, *Proceedings of the Forty-sixth Consecutive Constitutional Convention of the United Mine Workers of America, Pittsburgh, Pennsylvania, December 3–14, 1973*, p. 381.

3. "Miller Favors Teays Valley Site," *Charleston Gazette*, February 16, 1974, p. 1-A.

4. Ben A. Franklin, "Plan to Relocate UMW Fails Again," *New York Times*, March 16, 1974, p. 32.

5. "Miller Favors Teays Valley Site," p. 1-A.

6. UMW, *It's Your Union. Pass It On.: Officers' Report to the Forty-seventh Constitutional Convention, Cincinnati, Ohio, September, 1976*, p. 21.

7. Ben A. Franklin, "Two Years after His Election, Miners Criticize Miller," *New York Times*, January 25, 1975, p. 11.

8. Ibid.

9. Ibid.

10. Ben A. Franklin, "Challenge Foiled by UMW Leader," *New York Times*, February 12, 1975, p. 17.

11. Ibid.

12. "Notes on People," *New York Times*, August 12, 1975, p. 18, and "Yablonski Is Resigning Post as Mine Union Counsel," *New York Times*, August 13, 1975, p. 28.

13. Ben A. Franklin, "Miner Dissidents Open Convention," *New York Times*, May 28, 1972, p. 45, and Ben A. Franklin, "Reform Miners Select Candidate to Run against Boyle," *New York Times*, May 29, 1972, p. 14.

14. Ben A. Franklin, "Dissident Miners Rejected on Audit," *New York Times*, November 19, 1975, p. 11.

15. Ibid.

16. Ben A. Franklin, "Attempt to Depose Miller Is Made by Miners' Board," *New York Times*, November 4, 1975, p. 22.

17. Andrew Gallagher, "White Denies Voting for Miller's Ouster," *Charleston Gazette*, November 11, 1975, p. 5.

18. John P. Moody, "UMW's Miller Offers to Make Peace with Board and Trbovich," *Pittsburgh Post-Gazette*, November 26, 1975, p. 3.

19. "IEB Member Suspended," *UMW Journal*, January 1–15, 1976, p. 15.

20. "President Miller Visits Alaska to Protect Mine AMAX May Take Over," *UMW Journal*, January 16–31, 1976, p. 5.

21. "Trbovich Suspended by Miller for Refusing Organizing Duty in West," *UMW Journal*, April 16–31, p. 4.

22. "Trbovich Reinstated," *UMW Journal*, May 16–31, 1976, p. 4.

23. "A Special Message from President Miller," *UMW Journal*, April 1–15, 1976, pp. 2–3.

24. "Wildcat Strike Losses," *Charleston* (W. Va.) *Daily-Mail*, June 23, 1977, p. 1.

25. McAlister Coleman, *Men and Coal* (New York: Farrar and Rinehart, 1943), pp. 85–87, 94–104.

26. James Craft, "Transition in the Mine Workers Union and the Impact on Labor Relations," *Pittsburgh Business Review*, Summer 1976, p. 4.

27. James T. Wooten, "Coal Miners Close Their Own Union Offices in West Virginia as Wildcat Strike Enters Its Fourth Week," *New York Times*, August 27, 1975, p. 21.

28. Barbara Koeppel, "Why Miners Strike," *Progressive*, October 1976, p. 30.

29. Ibid.

30. Clark Kerr and Abraham Siegal, "The Interindustry Propensity to Strike," in Arthur W. Kornhauser, Robert Dubin, and Arthur M. Ross, eds., *Industrial Conflict* (New York: McGraw-Hill, 1954), pp. 189–212.

31. Keith Dix, "Wildcat Strikes: Vital Miners' Weapon," *Peoples Appalachia*, Winter 1972–73, p. 22.

32. Ibid.

33. Keith Dix et al., *Work Stoppages and the Grievance Procedure in the Appalachian Coal Industry* (Morgantown: West Virginia University Institute for Labor Studies), p. 80.

34. Ibid., p. 83.

35. Dix, "Wildcat Strikes," p. 22.

36. Ibid.

37. Dix, *Work Stoppages*, p. 54.

38. Koeppel, "Why Miners Strike," p. 29.

39. Ibid.

40. Ibid.

41. Ibid.

42. "Wildcat Strike Losses," p. 1.

43. "West Virginia's Wildcat Strikes," *Morgantown* (W. Va.) *Dominion-Post*, May 31, 1977, p. 12-A.

44. "Wildcat Strike Losses," p. 1.

45. UMW, *Officers' Report, 1976*, p. 35.

46. "Wildcat Strike Losses," p. 1.

47. John P. Moody, "UMW Health Benefits Slashed as Fund Dips," *Pittsburgh Post-Gazette*, June 18, 1977, p. 1.

48. Dix, "Wildcat Strikes," p. 25.

49. "Ten Thousand Miners End West Virginia Strike," *New York Times*, March 15, 1974, p. 38.

50. Ben A. Franklin, "Schools in Charleston to Reopen Despite a Growing Mine Protest," *New York Times*, September 17, 1974, p. 13.

51. Ben A. Franklin, "Miners Oppose Imports of Coal," *New York Times*, May 27, 1974, p. 32.

52. "Wildcat Strike Losses," p. 1.

53. "Thirty-three Mines Closed by Angry Workers," *New York Times*, February 19, 1975, p. 71. Data on strike from unpublished Bureau of Labor Statistics (BLS) source.

54. Data on strike from unpublished BLS source.

55. "Coal Miners Break Tradition, Return to Work Despite Pickets," *New York Times*, September 9, 1975, p. 20.

56. Andrew Gallagher, "Here's Account of Miners' Strike," *Charleston Gazette*, August 31, 1975, p. 12-C.

57. Ben A. Franklin, "Strike Challenging Reform Leadership of UMW," *New York Times*, September 7, 1975, p. 35.

58. "Most Miners in State Back on Job," *Charleston Gazette*, September 11, 1975, p. 10-C.

59. "Miller, Patrick Meet with W. Va. Local Officers to Plan Commission Hearings," *UMW Journal*, September 16–30, 1975, p. 3.

60. John P. Moody, "UMW Wildcat Disciplining Stirs Emotions," *Pittsburgh Post-Gazette*, October 19, 1975, p. 4.

61. "Wildcat Strike Losses," p. 1.

62. "Work Stoppages in 1976," *BNA Union Labor Report*, February 10, 1977, p. 6.

63. Ibid.

64. Rick Steelhammer, "Miners Threaten Strike Today," *Charleston Gazette*, March 1, 1976, p. 1-A.

65. Koeppel, "Why Miners Strike," p. 28.

66. Ibid.

67. "Work Stoppages in 1976," p. 6.

68. "A Courtroom Snarl over Wildcat Strikes," *Business Week*, August 30, 1976, p. 26.

69. "Almost Everyone Is the Victim," *Time*, August 9, 1976, p. 53.

70. Koeppel, "Why Miners Strike," p. 28.

71. "Almost Everyone Is the Victim," p. 53.

72. "Wildcat Strike Losses," p. 1.

73. UMW, *Officers' Report, 1976*, p. 1.

Chapter 5

1. "Call for the Forty-seventh UMWA Constitutional Convention," *UMW Journal*, May 16–31, 1976, pp. 6–7.

2. "Miller Appeals IEB Actions to Convention," *UMW Journal*, May 16–31, 1976, p. 3.

3. UMW, *Proceedings of the Forty-seventh Consecutive Constitutional Convention of the United Mine Workers of America, Cincinnati, Ohio, September 23–October 2, 1976*, p. 3.

4. Delegate figures from UMW, *Proceedings of the Forty-sixth Consecutive Constitutional Convention of the United Mine Workers of America, Pittsburgh, Pennsylvania, December 3–14, 1973*, pp. 448–63, and membership figures from UMW, *It's Your Union. Pass It On.: Officers' Report to the Forty-seventh Constitutional Convention, Cincinnati, Ohio, September 1976*, p. 3.

5. Delegate figures from UMW, *Proceedings of the Convention, 1976*, pp. 509–22, and membership figures from UMW, *It's Your Union*, p. 2.

6. The members per delegate quotient is found by dividing the total union membership by the number of delegates. It is a crude indication of how distant the functions of governance are from the membership.

7. Ben A. Franklin, "Mine Union Leader Opens a Parley," *New York Times*, September 27, 1976, p. A16.

8. Following are the numbers of pages of resolutions printed in the proceedings of UMW conventions from 1948 to 1976: 1948, 179; 1952, 314; 1956, 223; 1960, 276; 1964, 157; 1968, 279; 1973, n.a.; 1976, 1,500. Page and type size were approximately equal for each year.

9. UMW, *Proceedings of the Fortieth Consecutive Convention of the United Mine Workers of America, Cincinnati, Ohio, October 5–12, 1948*, vol. 2, pp. 3–71, and vol. 3, pp. 3–109.

10. UMW, *Resolutions to the Forty-seventh Consecutive Constitutional Convention of the United Mine Workers of America, Cincinnati, Ohio, September 23–October 2, 1976*, vols. 1, 2, and 3.

11. Interview with senior UMW staff members, October 1, 1976, Cincinnati, Ohio.

12. UMW, *Proceedings of the Convention, 1976*, p. 523.

13. UMW, *Proceedings of the Convention, 1973*, introduction.

14. UMW, *Proceedings of the Convention, 1976*, p. 523. IEB members holding committee positions were John Kelly, Frank Clements, Lonnie Brown, Nick DeVince, Karl Kafton, Robert Edney, and Andrew Morris.

15. UMW, *Proceedings of the Thirtieth Consecutive Constitutional Convention of the United Mine Workers of America, Indianapolis, Indiana, January 25–February 2, 1927*, p. 304.

16. This is an opinion arrived at through personal observation of the proceedings of the 1976 UMW convention.

17. UMW, *Proceedings of the Convention, 1976*, pp. 507–8.

18. UMW, *Proceedings of the Convention, 1973*, p. 191.

19. UMW, *Proceedings of the Convention, 1976*, Credentials Committee, amended report, pp. 215–18; Health and Safety Committee, amended report, pp. 219–33; Health and Retirement Committee, supplemental report, pp. 476–79; Collective Bargaining Committee, amended report, pp. 494–95; and Organizing Committee, amended report, pp. 495–99.

20. Ibid., pp. 20–21.

21. "Mine Union's Chief to Run Again in '77," *New York Times*, March 31, 1975, p. 28.

22. John Blosser, "Trbovich Might Run for Top UMW Office," *Morgantown* (W. Va.) *Dominion-Post*, December 31, 1975, section 2, p. 1.

23. UMW, *Proceedings of the Convention, 1976*, p. 3.

24. UMW, *Report to the Delegates of the 1976 UMWA Convention by Mike Trbovich, Vice-President*, text of speech handed to press, September 23, 1976, p. 11.

25. Ibid., p. 1.

26. UMW, *Proceedings of the Convention, 1976,* pp. 98–103.

27. Ibid., pp. 40–95.

28. UMW, *Proceedings of the Convention, 1968,* pp. 28–216.

29. UMW, *Proceedings of the Convention, 1976,* pp. 40–95.

30. Ibid., pp. 33–34.

31. "The Leaderless Miners Edge toward a National Strike," *Business Week,* October 11, 1976, p. 98.

32. UMW, *Proceedings of the Convention, 1976,* pp. 476–79.

33. Ibid., pp. 426–36.

34. Ibid., pp. 467–74.

35. Ibid., pp. 251–54.

36. Ibid., pp. 302, 342–44, 449–50.

37. Ibid., 548–60.

38. "Union Eyes Tough Contract Fight in '77," *UMW Journal,* October 1976, pp. 12–13.

Chapter 6

1. Press conference with Harry Patrick, Netherlands-Hilton Hotel, Cincinnati, Ohio, September 30, 1976.

2. Thomas N. Bethell, "UMW Election: Sound and Fury, But Is Anyone Listening?," *Coal Patrol,* June 1, 1977, p. 2.

3. "Mine Union's Chief to Run Again in '77," *New York Times,* March 31, 1975, p. 28.

4. "Miller Explains Ouster of Two U.M.W. Aides," *New York Times,* October 11, 1976, p. 16, and "Miller Says Charges 'Absurd,' " *Morgantown* (W.Va.) *Dominion-Post,* October 00, 1976, p. 00.

5. George Getschow, "UMW Chief's Firing of Two Aides Fuels Dissension; Actions May Be Challenged," *Wall Street Journal,* October 11, 1976, p. 2.

6. "UMW Ex-Aide Hits $16,000, Three-Page Study," *Washington Post,* October 8, 1976, p. B-6.

7. "Miller Explains Ouster of Two U.M.W. Aides," *New York Times,* October 11, 1976, p. 16.

8. "UMW Shakeup Widening," *Morgantown Dominion-Post,* October 28, 1976, p. 1.

9. "UMW Rift Widening; Probe of Patrick Set," *Morgantown Dominion-Post,* October 27, 1976, p. 3.

10. Getschow, "UMW Chief's Firing Fuels Dissension," p. 8, and George Getschow, "The Coal War's Hot at UMW Building Except on Fourth Floor," *Wall Street Journal,* December 22, 1976, p. 1.

11. Ibid.

12. Bill Peterson, "Miners' Infighting Paralyzing Union," *Rochester* (N.Y.) *Democrat and Chronicle,* January 30, 1977, p. 16A.

13. Getschow, "The Coal War's Hot," p. 1.

14. On the Bethell resignation, see, "The Mine Workers Lose More Staff as 1977 Bargaining Nears," *Wall Street Journal,* January 18, 1977, p. 1; on the Sparks resignation, see "UMW Is without a Press Officer," *Morgantown Dominion-Post,* January 4, 1977, p. 2; and on the Trumka resignation, see "Back to the Mines," *Rochester Democrat and Chronicle,* March 20, 1977, p. C-1. See also, "Survey Shows Miller's Major '72 Supporters Backing Patterson for Presidency in '77," Patterson campaign material in *UMW Journal,* May 1–15, 1977, p. 22.

15. Patrick revealed he was seriously considering challenging Miller at a December IEB meeting. Rick Von Sant, "UMW Split Can't Get Worse," *Morgantown Dominion-Post,* December 20, 1976, p. 1; "Patrick Announces Bid to Challenge Miller for UMW Presidency," *Wall Street Journal,* January 14, 1977, p. 2.

16. "Mine Union's Chief to Run Again in '77," p. 28.

17. During the proceedings of the 1976 UMW convention numerous buttons, stickers, and one-page leaflets promoting Patterson's candidacy were visible. Patterson made an effort to remain aloof from any such activity throughout the convention.

18. "Patrick Announces Bid to Challenge Miller for UMW Presidency," p. 2.

19. Bethell, "UMW Elections," p. 1.

20. John P. Moody, "UMW's Miller Names Re-Election Bid Slate," *Pittsburgh Post-Gazette,* December 22, 1976, p. 13, and Terry Pristin, "Miller Quarterbacking New UMW Team," *Morgantown Dominion-Post,* December 22, 1976, p. 3-A.

21. Ibid.

22. "Harry Patrick's Slate Is Qualified. No Other Candidate Can Make That Claim," Patrick campaign material in *UMW Journal*, May 16–31, 1977, p. 38.

23. Patterson campaign material, *UMW Journal*, April 1977, p. 12.

24. Interview with Mike Tamtom, candidate for vice president of UMW, June 4, 1977, at Fairmont (W. Va.) Holiday Inn.

25. "The Patrick Slate," Patrick campaign material in *UMW Journal*, May 1–15, 1977, p. 8.

26. UMW, UMWA Constitution, 1976, Article VI, Sections 2, 5, and 11.

27. "Official List of Candidates and Local Union Nominations," *UMW Journal*, April 1977, p. 11.

28. Ann Hughey, "Patterson Crowing over Nominations," *Charleston* (W.Va.) *Gazette*, March 20, 1977, p. 18.

29. UMW, UMWA Constitution, 1973, Article X, Section 7.

30. Hughey, "Patterson Crowing over Nominations," p. 18.

31. UMW, UMWA Constitution, 1976, Article VI, Section 11.

32. "A Message from the International Tellers," *UMW Journal*, April 1977, p. 11.

33. "Patterson Protest Denied as UMW Ballots Go Out," *Pittsburgh Post-Gazette*, May 28, 1977, p. 3.

34. Lawrence Leamer, "Tony Boyle, Arnold Miller, and the Ghost of John L. Lewis," *New York Times Magazine*, November 26, 1972, pp. 82–84.

35. Speech by Arnold Miller, May 30, 1977, at election rally held at the Cokesburg (Pa.) firehall.

36. Bethell, "UMW Election," p. 2.

37. Joseph Rauh, "Internal Union Problems: A Study of the United Mine Workers Union," *Proceedings of the 1973 New York University Conference on Labor*, June 8, 1973, p. 299.

38. Interview with Harry Patrick, UMW secretary-treasurer and presidential candidate, June 14, 1977, at Fairmont (W.Va.) Holiday Inn.

39. "Bathhouse Report," Patterson campaign material in the *UMW Journal*, May 16–31, 1977, p. 27.

40. "Be Proud You Are a Miner," Miller campaign material distributed at election rally held at Cokesburg firehall, May 30, 1977.

41. "Backers Snub Arnold Miller at Hill Party," *Morgantown Dominion-Post,* June 10, 1977, p. 1-A.

42. "Patterson Says Election Ballots Are Rigged," *Fairmont* (W. Va.) *Times-West Virginia,* June 5, 1977, p. 9A.

43. Patterson campaign material, *UMW Journal,* May 1–15, 1977, pp. 27–29.

44. Bethell, "UMW Election," p. 2.

45. David Ignatius and George Getschow, "Conflicts Flare Late in UMW Campaign, Adding New Uncertainty over Outcome," *Wall Street Journal,* June 6, 1977, p. 12.

46. "Patterson's Action Draws Criticism," *Charleston* (W. Va.) *Sunday Gazette-Mail,* May 7, 1977, p. 4A.

47. Patrick campaign material, *UMW Journal,* May 16–31, 1977, p. 32.

48. Interview with Harry Patrick, June 14, 1977.

49. "UMWA Election Special," *Coal Patrol,* June 16, 1977, p. 2.

50. "Survey Shows Miller's Major '72 Supporters Backing Patterson for Presidency in '77," Patterson campaign material in *UMW Journal,* May 1–15, 1977, p. 22.

51. UMW, *It's Your Union. Pass It On.: Officers' Report to the Forty-seventh Constitutional Convention, Cincinnati, Ohio, September, 1976,* p. 24.

52. Ira Fine, "Miller Gets Vital UMW Support," *Pittsburgh Press,* May 8, 1977, p. B-2.

53. Phil Primack, "Can Patrick Revive Reform in United Mine Workers?" *Whitesburg* (Ky.) *Mountain Eagle,* June 9, 1977, p. 26.

54. "Patrick Predicts Election Ouster, Long Court Battle," *Morgantown Dominion-Post,* June 29, 1977, p. 13-B.

55. "Miller Skips TV Debate with Two UMW Candidates," *Pittsburgh Post-Gazette,* June 6, 1977, p. 3, and "Patterson Tells It Like It Is as Miller Ducks Five Debates," Patterson campaign material, *UMW Journal,* June 1–15, 1977, p. 10.

56. For candidates' campaign materials, platforms, and positions, see, *UMW Journal,* April, May 1–15, May 16–31, and June 1–15, 1977.

57. "UMW Presidential Rivals Compared," *Charleston* (W.Va.) *Daily-Mail,* June 14, 1977, p. B-1.

58. Ibid.

59. Ibid.

60. "Patterson Team Lets You Know Their Goals," flyer distributed for Patterson campaign.

61. See Miller campaign material in *UMW Journal*, April, May 1–15, May 16–31, and June 1–15, 1977.

62. Primack, "Can Patrick Revive Reform?," p. 26.

63. "UMW Presidential Rivals Compared," p. B-1.

64. See Patrick campaign material in *UMW Journal*, April, May 1–15, May 16–31, and June 1–15, 1977.

65. Ibid.

66. "Results of the UMWA International Election," *UMW Journal*, July 16–31, 1977, p. 12.

67. Ibid.

68. Ibid.

69. "UMWA Election Special," pp. 2–3.

70. Ibid.

71. Based on discussions with miners throughout the campaign, particularly at Eastern Coal Company's Granttown, West Virginia, portal, June 17, 1977, and Patrick campaign headquarters, Fairmont Holiday Inn, June 14, 1977.

72. UMW, *Proceedings of the Forty-seventh Consecutive Constitutional Convention of the United Mine Workers of America, Cincinnati, Ohio, September 23–October 2, 1976*, pp. 203, 496–99.

73. "UMWA Election Special," p. 2.

74. Ann Hughey, "Miller Challenge Response Unsure," *Charleston Gazette*, June 28, 1977, p. 16-A.

75. John P. Moody, "UMW Aide Reports Bribe Offer," *Pittsburgh Post-Gazette*, July 22, 1977, p. 2.

76. "UMW Election Challenge Rejected," *Morgantown Dominion-Post*, July 22, 1977, p. 1.

77. "Labor Department Upholds Miller's Election," *UMW Journal*, October 1977, p. 3.

78. Ben A. Franklin, "Two Departures End an Era for Mine Union," *New York Times*, December 23, 1977, p. A14.

Chapter 7

1. Ben A. Franklin, "Two Departures End an Era for Mine Union," *New York Times*, December 23, 1977, p. A14.

2. Ibid.

3. Interview with Harry Patrick, UMW secretary-treasurer and presidential candidate at Fairmont, West Virginia, Holiday Inn, June 14, 1977.

4. Franklin, "Two Departures End an Era for Mine Union," p. A14.

5. Ibid.

6. "Patrick to Earn $36,000 in New Job," *Charleston* (W.Va.) *Gazette*, February 10, 1978.

7. John P. Moody, "UMW Health Benefits Slashed as Fund Dips," *Pittsburgh Post-Gazette*, June 18, 1977, p. 1.

8. George Getschow, "Coal Strikes Developing in Eastern U.S. over Medical-Benefit Cuts Slated July 1," *Wall Street Journal*, June 20, 1977, p. 5; John P. Moody, "Thirteen Thousand Strike West Virginia Pits, Protest Medical Aid Cut," *Pittsburgh Post-Gazette*, June 22, 1977, p. 1; and Suzanne Jaworski Rhodenbaugh, "UMWA Funds Problems," *Pittsburgh Post-Gazette*, July 13, 1977, p.8.

9. Frank P. Jarrell, "Patrick Urges Huge to Resign," *Bluefield* (W. Va.) *Daily Telegraph*, August 17, 1977, p. 1.

10. Getschow, "Coal Strikes Developing," p. 5.

11. Moody, "Thirteen Thousand Strike," p. 1.

12. Ann Hughey, "Ending Wildcat Strike to Get Full Attention, Miller Vows," *Charleston Gazette*, August 16, 1977, p.1, and Frank P. Jarrell, "All State Mines Reported Closed," *Bluefield Daily Telegraph*, August 5, 1977, p.1.

13. "Last Coal Miners Return to West Virginia Fields," *New York Times*, September 7, 1977, p. A18.

14. UMW, *Proceedings of the Forty-seventh Consecutive Constitutional Convention of the United Mine Workers of America, Cincinnati, Ohio, September 23–October 2, 1976*, pp. 382–405, 494–95, and 548–60.

15. Barbara Koeppel, "Why Miners Strike," *Progressive*, October 1976, p. 30.

16. Thomas N. Bethell, "UMWA and BCOA Agree to Fire Wildcat Strikers," *Whitesburg* (Ky.) *Mountain Eagle*, December 22, 1977, p. 1.

17. Ibid.

18. "Official Disputes Right-to-Strike," *Fairmont* (W.Va.) *Times–West Virginian*, November 29, 1977, p. 1.

19. Bethell, "UMWA and BCOA Agree to Fire Wildcat Strikers," p. 1.

20. "UMW, Coal Operators to Begin Labor Talks," *Wall Street Journal,* October 3, 1977, p.1.

21. Bethell, "UMWA and BCOA Agree to Fire Wildcat Strikers," p. 1.

22. "UMW's Miller Vows to Sit out Coal Talks Until Health-Fund Proposals Are Heard," *Wall Street Journal,* October 28, 1977, p. 6.

23. "Chaos in Coal's Labor Relations," *Business Week,* November 28, 1977, p. 92.

24. "UMW Negotiates for Lost Benefit," *Morgantown* (W.Va.) *Dominion-Post,* December 14, 1977, p. 12-B.

25. John P. Moody, "Coal Talks Resume Today in Washington," *Pittsburgh Post-Gazette,* December 8, 1977, p. 5.

26. John P. Moody, "Coal Talks Stalled, Union Isn't Ready," *Pittsburgh Post-Gazette,* October 7, 1977, p. 1.

27. "UMWA Assembles Team of Experts to Assist Bargaining Team," *UMW Journal,* September 16–30, 1977, p. 6.

28. "Federal Mediator Is in Hot Spot in Stalled Coal Talks," *Bluefield Daily Telegraph,* January 22, 1978, p. 8-C.

29. "Labor Letter," *Wall Street Journal,* January 3, 1978, p. 1.

30. Ben A. Franklin, "UMW President a Target of Both Sides," *New York Times,* February 17, 1978, p. D-11.

31. George Getschow, "UMW Chief's Firing of Two Aides Fuels Dissension; Actions May Be Challenged," *Wall Street Journal,* October 11, 1976, p. 8.

32. Strat Douthat, "Miller Appears Cast in a Trapped Role," *Beckley* (W.Va.) *Post Herald,* February 14, 1978, p. 1.

33. "Threats Made against Miller," *Fairmont Times-West Virginian,* February 10, 1978, p. 1.

34. Ann Hughey, "Ouster Reports 'Insult' to Miller," *Charleston Gazette,* December 3, 1977, p. 1, and Ben A. Franklin, "Coal Talks Dispute Focuses on Leaders," *New York Times,* December 2, 1977, p. B7.

35. Franklin, "Dispute Focuses on Leaders," B7.

36. Examples of this widespread coverage include a three-story feature by Rodney White, *Huntington* (W. Va.) *Herald-Dispatch,* November 18, 1977; a three-part series by Ann Hughey, *Charleston Gazette,* No-

vember 21, 22, and 23; and a story by Ben A. Franklin, *New York Times,* November 25, 1977.

37. Ann Hughey, "Coal Talks Break Down over Fines," *Charleston Gazette,* December 31, 1977, p. 1.

38. John P. Moody, "Coal Talks Resume, Individual Mine Strike Right Sought," *Pittsburgh Post-Gazette,* January 13, 1978, p. 7.

39. John P. Moody, "Coal Firms Mending Fences after Secret Talks Fail," *Pittsburgh Post-Gazette,* January 27, 1978, p. 2.

40. "Here's Summary of Coal Wage Agreement," *Charleston Gazette,* February 9, 1978, p. 12-A.

41. Ann Hughey, "Council Wants to See Contract Language," *Charleston Gazette,* February 8, 1978, p. 1.

42. George Getschow and Walter S. Mossberg, "President Moves to Ease Impact of Coal Walkout," *Wall Street Journal,* February 13, 1978, p. 2.

43. "Miller Blasts Pact Rejection: Says 90 Percent of Miners Back Offer," *Pittsburgh Press,* February 13, 1978, p. 1.

44. "Collapse of the Coal Pact," *Time,* February 20, 1978, p.75.

45. John P. Moody, "BCOA Requests Arbitration in Pact Snag with UMW," *Pittsburgh Post-Gazette,* February 22, 1978, p. 1.

46. "Coal Agreement Faces Uphill Battle for Ratification; Similar Pact at Pittsburg and Midway Soundly Rejected," *Wall Street Journal,* February 27, 1978, p. 3.

47. Ibid.

48. "The Coal Miners Decide," *Time,* March 13, 1978, pp. 10–13.

49. "The Miners Say No," *Newsweek,* March 13, 1978, pp. 24–26.

50. Urban C. Lehner and George Getschow, "Coal Miners Reject Proposed Pact as Carter Plans Move to End Strike," *Wall Street Journal,* March 6, 1978, p. 3.

51. Chambers Williams, "Were Miners Wrong?" *Charleston* (W.Va.) *Daily-Mail,* March 8, 1978, p. 1.

52. John P. Moody, "New Tentative Coal Pact Reached: UMW to Call Panel to Vote on Proposal," *Pittsburgh Post-Gazette,* March 15, 1978, p. 1.

53. Ibid.

54. "UMW Council Approves Pact," *Fairmont Times-West Virginian,* March 16, 1978, p. 1.

55. "Strike Legal Again; Miners Rage at Leaders," *Pittsburgh Press,* March 18, 1978, p. 1.

56. "Contract Ratified by 57 Percent Vote," *UMW Journal,* March 1978, p. 3.

57. "What Mine Contracts, Old and New, Contain," *Washington* (Pa.) *Observer-Reporter,* March 18, 1978, p. A6.

58. Ibid.

59. Ibid.

60. Karen Southwick, "Many Claim Miller Settled for 'Crumbs,' " *Morgantown Dominion-Post,* March 26, 1978, p. 2-A.

61. Ben A. Franklin, "In the Bitter Aftermath, Whither the UMW?," *New York Times,* March 26, 1978, sec. 4, p. 5.

62. "End-of-an-Era Clearance: Three UMW Cadillacs for Sale," *UMW Journal,* February 1, 1973, pp. 16–17, and "Notes on People," *New York Times,* January 4, 1978, p. C2.

63. "The Miller Team Isn't Just Arnold Miller," Miller campaign material, in *UMW Journal,* May 1–15, 1977, p. 13.

64. "Follow-up on the News," *Charleston Gazette,* January 4, 1978, p. 5-A.

65. "Notes on People," *New York Times,* January 4, 1978, p. C2.

66. "Miners to Miller: Shove It," *Workers Vanguard,* February 17, 1978, p. 1.

67. Matt Witt, "A Venture in Union Journalism," *Columbia Journalism Review* (July-August 1978): 50–52.

68. "Increase in Union Dues Facing Miners," *Clarksburg* (W. Va) *Telegram,* April 19, 1978, p. 1.

69. "Mine Workers Schedule Miami, Florida, Convention," *Wall Street Journal,* August 15, 1978, p. 35.

70. Robin Toner, "UMW Calls Forty-eighth Convention; Local Unions Begin Planning," *Charleston Daily-Mail,* June 21, 1979, p. 2.

71. UMW, UMWA Constitution 1973, Article IV, Section 6.

72. Salaries and expenses of UMW international officers from LM-2 reports on file with the Labor-Management Services Administration, U.S. Department of Labor, Washington, D.C.

73. Miners for Democracy, *The Miner's Voice,* June 1972.

74. "Miners to Miller: Shove It," p. 1.

75. "Labor Letter," *Wall Street Journal*, July 25, 1978, p. 1.

76. "UMW Board Rejects Petition to Oust Miller," *Wall Street Journal*, July 27, 1978, p. 19.

77. "UMW President: A Survivor Looking Back," *Morgantown Dominion-Post*, December 3, 1978, p. 2-G.

78. John P. Moody, "UMW's Miller Suffers Stroke," *Pittsburgh-Post Gazette*, March 30, 1978, p. 12.

79. "UMW Chief Miller Has Heart Attack," *Pittsburgh Post-Gazette*, April 13, 1978, p. 2.

80. "Arnold Miller Suffers from 'Exhaustion,' " *Morgantown Dominion-Post*, July 25, 1977, p. 4-A, "UMW President Taken to Charleston Hospital," *Morgantown Dominion-Post*, March 3, 1979, p. 2-A, and John P. Moody, "Will Step Down as UMW Chief Miller Says," *Pittsburgh Post-Gazette*, November 16, 1979, p. 2.

81. "Sam Church Jr., New Leader of United Mine Workers," *UMW Journal*, November 1979, p. 6.

82. John P. Moody, "Church Begins Task of Rebuilding UMW," *Pittsburgh Post-Gazette*, November 19, 1979, p. 1.

83. UMW, "Official Biography of Sam Church," June 1980.

84. Ben A. Franklin, "An Aggressive New Leader for Mine Union," *New York Times*, November 19, 1979, p. A-18.

Chapter 8

1. "Call for the Forty-eighth Consecutive UMWA Constitutional Convention," *UMW Journal*, July 1979, pp. 8–10.

2. UMW, "Convention '79 Fact Sheet," distributed to the press at Denver.

3. "Call for the Forty-eighth Convention," pp. 9–10.

4. The nine committees are the Credentials, Collective Bargaining, COMPAC/Legislative, Constitution and Grievances, Health and Retirement, Health and Safety, Organizing, Rules, and Resolutions Committees. The Health and Retirement Committee elects one active and one retired member from each district.

5. This observation was made by several committee members at the Denver convention.

6. UMW, *Resolutions Presented to the Forty-eighth Consecutive Constitutional Convention of the United Mine Workers of America, Denver, Colorado, December 10–20, 1979,* vols. 1 and 2.

7. Ben A. Franklin, "Innovation and Unity Mark Coal Union Convention," *New York Times,* December 17, 1979, p. A22.

8. UMW, *Partial Report of the Credentials Committee, 1979 UMW Convention, Denver, Colorado, December 10–20, 1979.*

9. UMW, *Proceedings of the Forty-eighth Consecutive Constitutional Convention of the United Mine Workers of America, Denver, Colorado, December 10, 1979,* p. 16.

10. Press conference with Sam Church, December 10, 1979, at Denver Convention Center.

11. UMW, UMWA Constitution, 1976, Article V, Section 2.

12. UMW, *Proceedings of the Convention, 1979,* December 11, 1979, p. 13.

13. Ibid., p. 15.

14. Ibid., p. 14.

15. Ibid.

16. Ibid., p. 16.

17. Ibid., p. 17.

18. Ibid., pp. 25, 36–37.

19. UMW, *Proceedings of the Forty-seventh Consecutive Constitutional Convention of the United Mine Workers of America, Cincinnati, Ohio, September 23–October 2, 1976,* pp. 426–36.

20. UMW, *Proceedings of the Convention, 1979,* December 11, 1979, pp. 17–20.

21. Ibid., pp. 31–32.

22. UMW, *Proceedings of the Convention, 1979,* December 12, 1979, p. 4.

23. Ibid., pp. 4–13.

24. Ibid., p. 9.

25. Ibid., pp. 15–43.

26. Ibid., pp. 3–4.

27. Thomas Petzinger, Jr., "Continental Oil Unit's Break with BCOA Clouds Future of Nationwide Coal Talks," *Wall Street Journal,* May 29, 1979, p. 5.

28. UMW, *Proceedings of the Convention, 1979,* December 13, 1979, pp. 28–30.

29. Ibid., p. 28.

30. Ibid., p. 30.

31. Ibid., pp. 18–22.

32. UMW, *Proceedings of the Convention, 1979,* December 17, 1979, pp. 49–52.

33. Strat Douthat, "Church Wins Some, Loses Some," *Valley News Dispatch* (Tarentum, Pa.), December 19, 1979, p. A-10.

34. Ibid.

35. UMW, *Proceedings of the Convention, 1979,* December 14, 1979, pp. 132–44, and UMW, *Report of the Collective Bargaining Committee, 1979 UMW Convention, Denver, Colorado, December 10–20, 1979.*

36. UMW, *Proceedings of the Convention, 1979.*

Chapter 9

1. "Patrick Charges Pennsylvania Miners' Trip Financed by UMW," *Charleston* (W.Va.) *Daily-Mail,* May 5, 1979, p. 1.

2. "Steel Union Editorial Attacks Victor Reuther as a Meddler," *New York Times,* August 12, 1976, p. 34.

3. Arnell Church, "Unemployment Continues to Surge," *UMW Journal,* August 1980, p. 30.

4. Strike figures from BCOA research department, August 1980.

5. George Crago, "Western Miners Earn $100 Daily; UMW Leaders Face New Pressures," *Morgantown* (W.Va.) *Dominion-Post,* June 19, 1977, p. 8-D.

6. Byron E. Calame, "Coal Miners May Walk Out in December, But Impact Won't Be What It Used to Be," *Wall Street Journal,* October 6, 1977, p. 44.

7. Press conference with Sam Church, December 12, 1979, Denver Convention Center.

8. William H. Miernyk, "Coal Industry Just Limping until the Big Day Arrives," *Charleston* (W.Va.) *Gazette,* April 29, 1978, p. 7A, and William H. Miernyk, "Crystal Ball Clouded on Decade's Coal Outlook," *Charleston Gazette,* February 24, 1980, p. 6J.

9. Excerpt from speech by Arnold Miller on record jacket of "Come All You Coal Miners," Rounder Records, 1973.

Index

187